HOW TO MANAGE
YOUR MOTHER

HOW TO MANAGE
YOUR MOTHER

UNDERSTANDING THE MOST DIFFICULT, COMPLICATED
AND FASCINATING RELATIONSHIP IN YOUR LIFE

ALYCE FAYE CLEESE
and BRIAN BATES

ARROW

Published by Arrow Books in 2003

3 5 7 9 10 8 6 4 2

Copyright © 1999, 2000 Alyce Faye Cleese and Brian Bates

Alyce Faye Cleese and Brian Bates have asserted their right under the
Copyright, Designs and Patents Act, 1988 to be identified and the
author of this work

First published in the United Kingdom in 2003 by Arrow

Arrow Books
The Random House Group Limited
20 Vauxhall Bridge Road, London, SW1V 2SA

Random House Australia (Pty) Limited
20 Alfred Street, Milsons Point, Sydney,
New South Wales 2061, Australia

Random House New Zealand Limited
18 Poland Road, Glenfield
Auckland 10, New Zealand

Random House (Pty) Limited
Endulini, 5a Jubilee Road, Parktown 2193, South Africa

The Random House Group Limited Reg. No. 954009

www. randomhouse.co.uk

A CIP catalogue record for this book
is available from the British Library

Papers used by Random House are natural, recyclable products made
from wood grown in sustainable forests. The manufacturing processes
conform to the environmental regulations of the country of origin

ISBN 0 09 945197 2

Printed and bound in Great Britain by
Bookmarque Ltd, Croydon, Surrey

Contents

Contents

Acknowledgments

We are very grateful to all of the following people for their help. Many of them generously gave us interviews about their mothers, on which this book is based, while others kindly advised and supported us through the various stages of research and writing.

Maria Aitken, Paddy Ashdown, Anne Askwith, Fay Ballard, Cliff Bates, Anne Beaumont, Jane Bedford, Mark Birley, Nancy Bresse, Nick Briggs, Roger Britnell, Guiseppe Bruno, Mike Burgh, Father Paul Byrne, Michael Caine, Helena Bonham Carter, Phoebe Cates, Henry Catto, Jessica Catto, Ming Chew, Wes Clark, John Cleese, Muriel Cleese, Jim Clubb, Marilyn Cole, Douglas Coupland, the crew of the *Seaborne Pride*, Jamie Lee Curtis, Richard Curtis, John Paul Davidson, Georgina Eyre, Richard Eyre, Nicole Farhi, Mia Farrow, Geoffrey Fine, Brenda Foguel, Philipe France, Emma Freud, Matthew Freud, Stephen Fry, Peter Gabriel, Dr. Yolonde Glaser, Jenny Goldman, William Goldman, John Goldwyn, Greg Gorman, Ian Gordon, Guy, Jamie Hambro, Rick Hambro, Rupert Hambro, David Hare, Douglas Hayward, Hugh Hefner, Gregory Hines, Lauren Hutton, Kay and Ann Jablownowski,

David Jones, Terry Jones, Kevin Kline, Wally Lamb, Peter Lattin, Mickey Lemle, Amy Lenzo, Lily the Drag Queen, Victor Lownes, Mike Marcardo, Steve Martin, Carmen McCracken, Susanne McDadd, David Mills, Nancy Mitchell, Pat Mounce, Dr. Mustafa, Liam Neeson, Mike Nichols, Ryan O'Connell, Brian O'Donnell, Terry O'Neill, Dwight Owsley, Jennifer Pade, Michael Palin, Mike Pierce, Patrick Plant, David Pogue, Carla Powell, General Colin Powell, Angela Rich, Keith Richards, Fiametta Rocco, Karl Sabbagh, Debbie Schindler, Richard Schmidt, Garry Scott-Irvine, Tom Selleck, Carla Santos Shamberg, Michael Shamberg, Kanwal Sharma, Mary Lou Shields, Sinbad, Robin Skynner, Kathleen Smith, Colonel Bill Smullen, Ed Soloman, Stephen Sondheim, Arianna Stassinopoulos Huffington, Agape Stassinopoulos, Marolyn Stewart, Miriam Stoppard, Carol Kaye Taylor, Todd Thayler, Mike Trace, two airline pilots over the Grand Canyon, Laurens van der Post, Maggie Wall, Michael Winner, Gertrude York.

Introduction

A book about mothers? Hardly a revolutionary idea, is it? But this book may be more unusual than you would expect—partly because it is written in entirely nontechnical language, but mainly because it is about *adults* and their mothers.

When I (Alyce Faye Cleese) started seeing patients as a psychotherapist many years ago, it did not surprise me, after all my psychoanalytic training, to find that they talked about their mothers a great deal! But I believed, at that time, that it was mainly artists and people who had sought therapeutic help who talked so much about their relationship with their mothers.

I was wrong. Gradually over the years I realized that all the people who told me about themselves focused on their mothers. So often when I fell into conversation at dinners, at cocktail parties, on trains, in airplanes, in social situations of all kinds, out the subject came. It seemed as though there was a button just below the heart, which, when pushed, caused an outpouring, a stream of consciousness—almost a confession—about mothers. And I also realized that relatively few of these people told me that their relationship with their mother was really good. Even when clearly they loved their mother, they usually seemed to have problems with her.

In a perfect world, as our childhood ended we would separate from our mothers psychologically and move on to a mature relationship in which we would communicate with our mothers as adults. But it seems that this is rarely achieved in real life. Most people have told me the opposite: how childlike or childish they sometimes felt in the presence of their mother, as though this relationship was somehow stuck in time, with the result that they could not escape from this outdated pattern into something more appropriate for an adult. They felt also that their mother was always criticizing them and that they could not please her; that she interfered in their lives too much; that she said they did not see her often enough or call frequently enough; or that they did not love her.

These issues seemed to me so important, so crucial to our lives, that I began to wonder if there was a way of writing a book from a fresh perspective that might help people to gain insight into their relationship with their mothers and help them get along better with them.

I discussed the project with a close friend and colleague, Brian Bates, who teaches and writes from the perspective of humanistic psychology. He too had found the issue of mothers to be central to many people's lives, and felt that there was a need for a book dealing with adults and their mothers. We agreed to research and write it together.

We were convinced that the fresh approach we were looking for would stay close to the experience of the people we wanted to help. So we decided to interview a wide range of people on their experiences with their mothers—not my patients or

Brian's students, but people specially interviewed for the book. We devised a set of standard questions to give the interviews structure (which is included in the appendix at the back of the book in case you would like to answer the questions for yourself). I interviewed more than a hundred people in depth, and a further group completed a questionnaire. These interviewees ranged from close friends to total strangers, in all sorts of occupations, aged twenty to ninety-eight, mainly in Europe and North America. Their stories form the basis of this book.

Many of the people we interviewed have allowed us to include their real names in the narrative. The stories are not invented case studies to illustrate existing theory, as is so often the case, but from the research data from which we have derived the ideas of the book. All the people who gave us interviews, whether or not we used their particular stories in the narrative, contributed to the data pool, and we are most grateful for their help. In some cases, where our interviewees' accounts touch on events or express opinions that might hurt the feelings of or offend their mothers, we have replaced their name with a pseudonym. The people who gave interviews are listed in the acknowledgments; names mentioned in the book but not in the acknowledgments are pseudonyms for the people listed there.

When we had compiled the interviews, Brian and I immersed ourselves in the stories and the meaning which, rather like folk tales and great fairy stories, they seemed to carry.

Clear themes began to emerge:

- many people receive much of their mothering from women other than their mothers

- the sacrifices mothers make are an important part of how we see them
- our feelings of guilt about the sacrifices they made cause rifts in many of our relationships with our mothers
- our efforts to meet our mothers' expectations are often misconceived, because they do not expect from us what we think they do
- secrets which mothers tried to keep from us during our childhood play a surprisingly influential role in our lives
- our attitude toward our mother's eventual death seems to go through quite distinct phases

Because of our belief that most of us, even when we love our mother, have some problems with her, our aim has been to use these stories, and the themes they reveal, to understand better our relationship with our mother, and to present ideas about what we can do to improve that relationship. If you feel frustration with some aspects of your relationship with your mother and want to do something about it, this book is for you.

We have found that in "managing" our mother it is best not to wrestle directly with current areas of dispute with her, but rather to concentrate on how we feel about the many remembered experiences we have from our shared past; in other words, to reexamine the fundamental way we think about her and about ourselves. Thinking through our attitudes to our experiences seems to affect our behavior deeply and directly and so leads to a closer and more positive relationship with our mother—much more so than trying to get her to change or making new resolutions to behave better toward her ourselves.

In writing the book, we wanted to let the interviews

speak for themselves, to use the stories to carry the ideas we wished to convey. For this reason the book is anecdotal. We realize that some of our professional colleagues might wish for more psychoanalytic theory or empirical research literature; but we believe that telling stories is more likely to affect our readers' emotions, and therefore their attitudes and behavior, than merely giving them information for their intellects.

It felt awkward to keep referring to "we," especially since I have also introduced quite a few experiences I had with my own mother and with other people. Brian and I have therefore written the book together, drawing on both our researches in psychoanalysis and psychology and our professional experience, but from my viewpoint, to make it a better and easier read.

We have necessarily concentrated on our problems with our mother. But this is not a "mother-blaming" book; on the contrary. We know many excellent mothers and believe that almost all mothers are very good in some ways. We hope this book will help to repay some of the good work a mother does by helping her adult children to understand her better and to have an improved relationship with her as a result.

1 SHE LOVES ME

Because the summers were so hot in Oklahoma, where I lived as a small child, my parents would get up in the cool of the dawn to work in their garden. When the rays of the early morning sun began to slant across the fields, my mother would come indoors to wake me. I remember clearly, as she leaned over my bed, the sweet smell on her of roses, and the earth, and the dew. She smelled so good. Happy memories like this are like the best days of summer: warm and bright.

Our earliest recollections of our mother, whether good or bad, tend to be made up of such sensual fragments; these images of how she looked, what she felt like, the sound of her voice, and her aroma, are wrapped together in our memory with a "feeling tone," a sense of the original emotion that we felt at the time. As we grow up, these memories and feelings gradually build up, in our heart and mind, into the attitude toward our mother that we have as an adult. This attitude is like a guiding image, and it is absolutely crucial in determining how we get along with her today. For this reason rediscovering our memories of her and understanding our feelings about them is the key to unlocking the door to a better relationship with our mother.

Understanding Early Memories

Of course, our relationship with our mother is about *today*. But it is a relationship that's different from any other in our life. She was the very first person we formed a relationship with, and that relationship continued all the way through our childhood to the emotional roller coaster of adolescence and beyond. Therefore, everything to do with us and our mother now is infused with this shared past, a history that colors the present with everything from the warm hues of love to the dark shadows of trouble.

All of us have both happy and sad memories of times spent with our mother, although since happiness presents us with no issues to wrestle with and no problems to solve, happy recollections do not stay with us as persistently as negative memories. Even those of us who get along well with our mother usually suffer some painful legacies: misunderstandings, wrong things said, right things unsaid, heated arguments, and, for some of us, frustrations, regrets, and bitter feelings toward her.

No matter where we fall on this scale of emotional response, there are ways we can improve our relationship with our mother. But how do we go about accomplishing this?

Many self-help books present their maxims as if we could read them one day and start living differently the next. But we are not machines that are simply in need of missing nuts and bolts. We are complex, organic beings, and for the lessons of a book to really make a difference to our life they must connect with us deeply. The stories and ideas of a book need to resonate with us, like a piece of music, for the medium of the psyche is akin to music; and in trying to improve our relationship with our mother we are trying to recompose the lyrics and retune that relationship.

We need, therefore, to begin not by calling to our minds all the problems, the blocks or the frustrations, but by establishing first a positive resonance with our mother. We can do this by recalling some happy experiences with her.

Starting with Happiness

I asked my interviewees for their earliest pleasant memories of their mother. Their responses, often no more than sound bites, give a feeling, a taste, a sniff, the barest glimpse of the origins of the positive aspects of their present view of her:

> "Looking up into her face. A feeling of love that came from her."
>
> "I remember her wonderful teeth and a huge smile."
>
> "A woman bustling around the kitchen, singing."
>
> "A woman with lots of curly hair."
>
> "Perfume."
>
> "My mother was a jumper. I remember her always jumping into action."
>
> "On a beach, in the sand, mother in the sixties, in a bikini."
>
> "With my mother, a sudden gust of wind, it was raining leaves, and I was very happy."
>
> "She had very pale skin, red lips, and very dark long hair. She always reminded me of Snow White."
>
> "Climbing into her bed; I remember the smell of her skin."
>
> "In a baby chair, being fed by my mother, and me refusing to eat my vegetables. I would only eat flying vegetables; they had to have wings."

Some early pleasant memories are fuller, like Carla Santos Shamberg's description of being with her mother at the beach. "We lived in New York City," she said. "But my mother loved the ocean, and she would take me there. My fondest memory is that she would carry me in her arms into the water, and we would jump the waves together for what would seem like hours. It was wonderful. I don't know if you have ever jumped waves, but you feel them all night long in your sleep."

Jane Bedford's warm memories of her mother were poignant: "When my dad had his stroke, we were living with my mom in public housing; the house had wooden floors. On Saturday mornings, she would let us kids polish the floor by tying dust rags on our feet, skating on the floor with the polish, and then again with dry dust rags to shine it up. Scooting along the floor, we loved that." Although this pleasant memory is colored by knowledge of her parents' later problems, children often instinctively understand much about the adult world even when they do not understand all the details. Even at her young age, Jane knew that her mother was having a difficult time, yet she still allowed Jane to have fun.

Some memories we can see, in retrospect, as starting points for pathways through our lives. David Pogue remembered the sound of his mother's voice. "My earliest memories of her are of being soothed. You know, I would be scared, or have hurt myself, and so my mother would sing to me." He recalled being taken as a small child on car trips, and his mother and father would sing. "They would sing duets on these car rides to pass the time, and we'd be in the backseat just rapt, listening to their harmonies." As a three- or four-year-old, David began to write his own songs: "My mother would write the songs down and make me feel like they were important. I had baby books full of these couplets. And now today, I'm a songwriter."

David's pleasant sense of being soothed by his mother's singing, and by her supporting his first efforts at musical creativity, form a "memory cluster," a scene or series of scenes, together with a sense of the original emotion about them that binds the images together.

Recovering memories, especially of our early childhood, helps us to understand how our present relationship with our mother has come about; it identifies the old, deep seams that bind us together. Throughout this book, we shall explore ways of unweaving our memories—a process that will free us from the strands of shared personal history that may have tied up our relationship in knots.

You may have memories like these of your mother—of having sensual pleasure or having fun or being encouraged. A surprising number of apparently lost memories are in fact readily accessible to us if we concentrate on recalling them, and you may wish to do this for yourself. The easiest technique is simply to sit in a quiet space and allow your relaxed mind to be open to images. Picture the places where you lived and the things you did together. Looking at old photographs is a good prompt for bringing back memories. Talking to people who knew you when you were young can fill in many details. Once you have stirred the pools of memory, images may bubble to the surface of your mind of their own accord, either during the day or in your dreams. It may be useful to start a memories notebook, as if you were writing an autobiography of your relationship with your mother, to keep these recollections from slipping back into the depths of your mind.

Burying Memories in Our Unconscious

Of course, we all have thousands of memories about our mother that we simply cannot recall. These are buried in our unconscious, either because they are too trivial or because they are too important. Memories seething with potent emotions are sometimes too disturbing for us to deal with, and our mind protects us by making them difficult to recall, keeping them under emotional lock and key. We remember them only when the doorway is pried open by some particular event.

That is what happened to Paddy Ashdown. "I must have been about three years old," he said, referring to the days of his early childhood, when he lived with his parents in India. "We were coming down from our house in the hills to the boat for the last time, because we were going home to England. The train stopped outside a station and, even though I remember my mother's presence close to me, I could feel fear, a sense of fear that recurred in my nightmares for a very long time. For some reason the train stayed there for what seemed to me, as a young child, like an eternity. Then it pulled slowly through the station and there was a terrible, acrid, pungent smell in the air. There on the platform, as I can still recall in my mind's eye, was dismembered body after dismembered body, covered in blood; there had been a massacre of either Hindus by Muslims or Muslims by Hindus." This appalling recollection was then lost to Paddy's unconscious for decades, buried deep in a place safe from disturbing his conscious mind. But it came back to him suddenly, twenty years later, when he was in the armed forces, fighting in Borneo: "I suddenly recognized something and then remembered that smell—the smell of decomposing bodies and my mother's presence at that time."

Repression is the term we apply to the process of hiding those elements of our past that we do not want to deal with, by concealing them under the cloak of our unconscious. It can be extremely revealing and valuable to explore such deep memories of incidents with your mother, whether they arise spontaneously, as Paddy's did, in response to some cue, or in dreams. Throughout the book we will give examples of how this can be done when dealing with a wide variety of issues with our mother.

Memory Is a Tricky Business

Memory is a tricky business. Recollections flash through our mind like quicksilver; the images are crystallized into a shape by the fire of emotion. But the recollections are not fixed and unchanging "facts"; as the years pass, these clusters of image and emotion evolve. They are formed of our original experience, but we continually "update" them, subtly altering details and the emotion attached to them so that the memories of our past are unconsciously shaping to fit the person we are today.

The way this works, deep in our mind, is that we link together the clusters in which our memories are stored in such a way that they form a complex attitude toward our mother. As our overall image of our mother takes shape, we process the events of our life and store our memories to fit this overall attitude. By the time we are adult, we have perpetuated our view of our mother, and the relationship becomes rigid. Problems between us cannot then be resolved.

But when we begin to examine our recollections of our mother closely, we find that they are malleable. That is not to say that the original memories are false; but what we thought were the "facts" of our past may turn out to be only a version of what happened to us, a "take" on our experiences with our mother which we fixed in our mind long ago. As long as these memories stay fixed, we are locked into an attitude, a general feeling, a guiding image of our mother that makes it difficult to change our relationship with her today. But when we recall and reexamine our memories, we realize just how constructed they are by our guiding image. So they can be deconstructed, and when we do this, our feelings about the event and our mother can change also. This is why reconsidering our shared personal history with our mother can make an enormous difference to the way we get along with her.

It might help to describe a couple of examples of how our guiding image of our mother can "fix" memories. Penny Charles has a distressing and difficult relationship with her mother. She was hurt by the way she felt she was treated by her mother, and has not had loving feelings toward her for as long as she can remember. But recently she saw a long-lost home movie from her childhood, showing her at age three or four. She was shocked by what she saw. "There is a moment when I'm dancing," she explained. "I'm holding a favorite Raggedy Ann doll and one of my mother's hats. I turn to the camera at one point, and I'm mouthing silently, 'I love you, Mommy.' It was so shocking for me to see, because I thought that I'd never loved my mother. What is that about? It was as if I were watching another person rather than myself."

For this young woman, the independent evidence of the film was deeply significant. "I cannot now trust my memory of events and feelings about my mother," she confessed.

However, such a realization may also be hopeful. In showing the extent to which we revise our original emotional memory in the light of subsequent experience, it suggests that this process may be reversible. If we can unravel the ways we have bound together our memories and emotions, we may be able to get closer to how we interacted with our mother originally. This is the single most important key to seeing our mother in a different light. Seeing her today without the distorting mirrors of years of reconstructed memories clearly enhances the opportunity for developing a better relationship with her.

We might assume that memories of our mother we formed later, when we were adolescents or young adults, are processed in a more mature manner, less shaped by our guiding image of our mother and therefore more reliable. But we would be wrong, as Stephen Sondheim discovered when he came across a couple of letters that he had written to his mother at the age of twenty. Their positive tone surprised him: "They are not full of gushing warmth, but they are not what my memory tells me I felt about her, either. They are much friendlier than that. My memory is that I hated her all my teenage years, but there's a lie there, someplace."

Reexamining our memories does not deny negative, painful, and upsetting aspects of our past with our mother, but it may release us from feelings about her that have become stuck like glue deep inside us. Realizing that our memories are always being revised opens the way for a fresh and more flexible start to this all-important relationship.

Guiding Images of Our Mother

In the next chapter we will consider ways of changing our relationship with our mother by thinking through our memories. But first, let us look more closely at the guiding images of our mother, the overall attitudes that play a large part in our ongoing relationship with her. All through our life, our experiences with our mother compete to shape this overall image. Good, happy, warm, positive, supportive experiences with her contribute to an overall image of "Mother is good"; whereas bad, cold, negative, critical ones build an overall image of

"Mother is bad." Most of us have a guiding image of our mother that is between these two extremes.

Many of these images are formed in childhood. For example, when I was five, I started taking piano lessons. The lessons were given at my teacher's home and, when the afternoon lesson was finished, she would let me play in the tree outside the house until my mother came to collect me. My mother had a propensity to try to cram too many things into one hour, and could be late for things. For some reason, on one particular day, my mother was quite late. It is hard to say how late, but it seemed like an eternity, and I decided that she was lost and gone forever. By the time my mother arrived, I was racked with heavy sobs and tears. I remember she just scooped me up and held me, and it felt so good. As a child, I had trusted my mother not to abandon me, and after my short period of doubt, she had confirmed that I was right all along. It made me feel that she was a good mother.

On the other hand, Jane Bedford had a different experience. Her brother, eighteen months older than she, had been diagnosed with cerebral palsy and was held back from starting school until Jane was old enough to go with him. "He was five and a half and I was four. When I started, he just did half days and I did whole days. On one occasion, I got into trouble at school, and the teacher made me go and stand outside the classroom door. Then I saw my mother arriving to pick up my brother to go home at lunchtime. So because she was there with him, and they were going home, I thought I could go home too. But she said quite severely, 'No, you have to keep standing where you are.' I remember seeing them going off home together, and I was so upset. I could not understand how she could possibly be on the side of the teacher, the one who was making me stand outside, because I thought that when my mother turned up, everything would be all right. It was a big shock to discover that it wasn't, that she was party to these strange rules." Jane felt her mother had abandoned her, and it created a sense that she was a bad mother.

Good and bad are not the only dimensions in which we respond to our mother, but there are fewer dimensions than we might think. Our emotional life does not elaborate things in the same way that our conscious thinking does. Feelings, after all, emanate from a more primitive area of the brain and are disseminated around our body by hormones, which produce the thrill of happiness, the uncomfortable jag of anxiety, the paralysis of fear, or the warm glow of love. Our guiding image of our mother is essentially an emotion, not an intellectual theory. That emotion produces a feeling tone (to return to the musical metaphor of our psyche). If it is a positive tone, we interpret things she does and says today in the best possible light, even if they are not really as good as we imagine. If it is a negative tone, then even when she is being supportive and cooperative, we think the worst of her, looking for hidden motives for her behavior. In this way we invent a kind of caricature of her, an exaggerated version in which we distort the facts. These images are of a type of mother rather than of a real mother. While these guiding images are very powerful, they are formed quite simply and, fortunately, they can be changed as a result of insight, of realizing how and why they are as they are.

An image of a good mother might store up problems for us, because to persistently see our mother in a better light than she deserves may mean that we are afraid of her, dependent on her, or unable to see how she is manipulating our life; but it is usually much less of a problem than an image of a bad mother. An extremely negative guiding image may be based on quite accurate assessments of aspects of our mother's character, but it may prevent us from opening our eyes to her best qualities.

Since we will explore negative experiences and images of our mother in the next chapter, let us continue to concentrate here on examples of positive images. In doing so, we should recognize that for those of us who have painful relationships with our mother, it can be difficult to read about people who feel they have supportive and loving relationships with their mother, but the aim of looking at these examples is to help us identify—and relate to—the positive aspects of our mother.

"Good mother" images result from childhood experiences of our mother's love that are taken into our internal world, into our imagination, where they form an idealized image of her in which her love seems always available to us and feels unconditional. Such an image is not an objective judgment of her whole character but takes on great importance as a touchstone and becomes the symbol of our mother—even when we are adults.

"I don't remember me without my mother," Arianna Huffington declared. "I have a very symbiotic relationship with her. My earliest memory of her is my earliest memory of me." This feeling of closeness, of being bound up with a mother, is characteristic of adults who have a good mother image. (People who have difficulties with their mother often, as we shall see, feel a *distance,* a sense of a gap that cannot be closed.)

"I feel that she has this incredible gift," Arianna continued. "It's the greatest gift a mother can have—of unconditional loving. She really, truly, loves me unconditionally. It's affected everything about me. She's given me security, because I always feel loved by her, no matter what else has been going wrong."

Unconditional love is perhaps everyone's greatest desire: the knowledge that we will be loved no matter what we do, and that whatever happens that love will not be withdrawn. For some people this idea of unconditional love seems an unacceptable notion—utopian, sentimental, and wholly unrealistic. For when we try consciously to commit ourselves to it, as when in a traditional marriage ceremony we promise to love forever, we learn just how difficult it is to sustain amid the rough and tumble of our emotional lives. Nevertheless, I am certain, both from the evidence of my interviews and my psychotherapeutic practice and from knowing many mothers, that the love some mothers have for their children *can* be unconditional. It can be unshakable, no matter what happens. So a guiding image of our mother as loving us unconditionally can be rooted in reality.

Being loved unconditionally in this way by our mother does not necessarily mean that we are indulged or spoiled, that she never gets angry with us, or that she does not sometimes disapprove of what we do. A mother who loves her child unconditionally may draw boundaries, discipline, and indeed punish when she feels it is appropriate. But there is something deeper present, an enduring positive emotion that seems unaffected by transient disapproval.

Such an image can give us enormous emotional strength, as Arianna Huffington's experience shows—an example of how self-confidence stems from feeling loved by our mother and knowing that that love is secure.

As a small child, Nick Briggs lived with his family in one of the oldest houses in New South Wales, Australia. It had a huge and ancient electric oven. One day, while his mother was preparing to roast a chicken, Nick suddenly swung on the open oven door, and the whole oven came out of the wall and fell on top of him. "My mother and the cleaning lady saw me under this huge oven, and they lifted it up, and I was rushed to the hospital. I'd fractured my pelvis. Later it took four men to move that oven. And yet my mother and the cleaning lady, a tiny little woman, had picked it up. It was the power of love."

Nick's guiding image is that of mother as heroine. If we are in trouble, she will rescue us, and there are no limits to her powers. The feeling that our mother can save us from disaster generates security and the sure knowledge that we can ask for help.

"When I was anxious as a kid, my mom would stay up all night listening to me ranting about God knows what, and she would never complain," Marilyn Cole said. "She would never say, 'Look, I've got to get to work in the morning.' And I remember sometimes saying, 'Will you come out in the garden with me? I need to walk and talk.' This was in the middle of the night! And she would!"

The importance of our mother's listening to us is more than in merely her hearing our accounts of life's traumas or giving us advice. It is the being there with us, uncritically, that gives us the sense that our dilemmas are understood and shared. It is the nonjudgmental nature of this listening that makes it so special. Most of us have had some experience of our mother's listening to us in this way. Even in a difficult relationship, there may have been moments when she was able to put aside her own anxieties and worries, attend to us in a supportive way, and listen lucidly. But an image of a mother who is always available, always uncritical, is a guiding image. It would be almost impossible for any woman really to be totally "there" for her child every time without completely sacrificing her own life in the process.

Sometimes a good mother image can be formed quite late. Nicole Farhi did not really appreciate her mother's listening to her until she grew up. This is not unusual, for there is no childhood checklist that says, "This is mother love and you should recognize it as such."

"If I think about my dad, he was warm, generous, loving, cuddly," Nicole said. "My mother is not. My mother is very intelligent and very bright. She understands things that are not said. She's intuitive. She was not someone I would go to for a cuddle—for that I would always go to my father. But she was the one I would go to to discuss things that were bothering me and big issues in my life."

So Nicole appreciated her mother as a good listener, but this did not feel like love, because the warmth came from her father. "My father was love, and my mother was understanding. I fought my mother when I was young, because at times I just wanted to be loved. I didn't want to have to explain myself, whereas she wanted to understand every little thing about my behavior."

As Nicole grew older, the balance of her relationships with her parents changed, as it does for many of us. The crucial episode was when Nicole wanted to go to Paris to study fashion design. At this point her father's love for her became restricting. He could not understand why she wanted to go to Paris and did not want her to leave. "I used to overhear them when they were talking at night. My mother was the one who insisted, 'You have to let her go.'"

The realization changed her view of her mother. "I still had not appreciated my mother much up until then. It was only during the six months before I left, when she was fighting my father to let me go to Paris, that I realized how wonderful she was, and what a help she was in my life."

What she had felt as love from her father had now become overwhelming and smothering. The love of her mother, previously experienced as rather distant, now seemed healthier. She could accept Nicole's autonomy and independence, so that she could explore, yet stay supported by her family. A mother who listens and understands is a mother who loves you. When Nicole finally realized this, she found she had formed a positive guiding image—of a mother who loves her by understanding.

When we are very young, we experience our parents as omnipotent beings; especially our mother, with whom we are likely to spend the most time. She seems to us all-powerful; she can act to change the basic, all-consuming dimensions of our infant experiences, either by giving us what we want, or by "failing" us. The feelings about her that we form early on in our lives are established at a very deep level and are rarely discarded completely. They shape our guiding image of our mother.

The images we have seen of the mother who loves us unconditionally may be more or less real, because, of course, mothers are human, with all the strengths and failings that we know and recognize in all humans. We do not expect our mother, even the best of them, to unfailingly reach these heights every single day of her life. But we can take the best elements of our mother by recalling happy experiences with her and identifying her positive qualities, and create from them an image of her that can sustain us throughout our life.

2 SHE LOVES ME NOT

When something hap-

pens to us that we intensely dislike, the emotion

we experience seems to serve as a flame that car-

bonizes and fixes the memory of it in our psyche.

The incident stays with us, vivid and unchanging,

for years, decades, or even a lifetime. Both positive and negative experiences do this, but the latter burn a deeper trace and influence more strongly the way we behave toward our mother today.

If we feel unloved by our mother, we often form negative images and carry as adults an internalized attitude toward her that can run the gamut from feeling ambivalent, critical, negative, and hostile, all the way to outright hatred of her. We have seen in chapter 1 that our memories are stored in such a way as to support our general attitude toward our mother. When our recollections are examined closely they may begin to change shape, and our feelings about the original event, and our mother, may change also. So learning to manage our relationship with our mother entails recovering and examining those memories that contributed to our negative guiding image of her. In doing this, we need to fully acknowledge and accept that our negative memories can be painful; but the process is an essential step to healing the wounds of rejection and building a better relationship with our mother.

"My Mother Doesn't Understand Me"

We expect our mother to understand us. If she does not, we naturally feel hurt and form a negative image of her, as Bill Goldman did: "I have no fond memories of my mother in any way, shape, or form," he said.

During his high school years Bill, in his own estimation, was "amazingly inept socially." He had almost no friends, struggled painfully through adolescence, and never dated. He had one saving grace: he loved sports and was a very good tennis player. "We belonged to a country club, which I hated except for the tennis courts," he said. "So I would go to the courts, play, go home, and never go into the club." This routine worked well for Bill, until his mother stepped in to give him a "treat." "The night of my fourteenth birthday, my mother gave a surprise party for me at the country club. It was one of the worst nights of my life. There were all these poor damned kids who didn't know me or didn't like me and didn't want to be there. And I don't dance. My brother was so fat that he couldn't dance, and I wasn't allowed to surpass my brother."

The party seemed a travesty of understanding for such a social loner as young Bill.

"At the end of the evening, I said to my mother, 'Marion, that was so terrible. Don't you understand? It was just horrible. It was an awful embarrassment.' And she said, 'I am so sorry, I thought that once we got into it you would enjoy it. I am so sorry.' But the next year she did it again. That is the real point. If you want to know what my mother was really like, it was the second surprise party, the *identical* arrangements the second year."

How do we begin to come to terms with experiences like the one Bill describes and the damaging negative images of our mother that result? If we are to have the chance to move beyond the inevitable knot of emotion that binds such an event in our psyche, the memory needs to be unwoven and new perspectives found. First we have to face how we feel now—the sadness, bitterness, and anger that well up when dark elements of our past enter our imagination. These feelings are natural, and while we must process them and transcend them before we can think about our mother in a more positive way, the hurt of the original experience may stay with us for a long time.

But the fact that changing the way we think also tends to change both the way we feel and the way we subsequently act or behave reveals a central truth: managing our mother is largely about managing ourselves. We have to let go of the "hurt victim" scenario, which was appropriate as a child and understandable as a young adult, but is inappropriate now. This is not easy, for a victim perspective gives us permission to feel sorry for ourselves, and that serves as a mild balm for the wound. But this perspective will not heal anything. The reward of letting go and achieving a mature vision of our experiences with our mother is a better relationship with her.

In order to find a new perspective on the sort of experience Bill has described, we need to remember that there is no really objective truth; all situations between mother and child are complex, and a mother's recollection of the same event might be quite different from her child's. For example, Bill admitted that he was a shy and lonely adolescent. A sensitive and loving mother would, we assume, have paid attention to this fact and planned a birthday celebration more appropriate for such a child. Not to have done so seems like poor mothering, and hurtful for Bill. But we may be able to conceive of positive motives for what she did. It is possible, for example, that Bill's mother thought that a large party at the country club would raise his profile and status among his peers. She may have thought that a healthy and happy teenager ought to enjoy such parties, and that if she kept providing them he would eventually become more socially confident and more at ease with being the center of attention.

It sometimes helps us to reach a new perspective if we remember that we all played our role in those painful scenarios. Perhaps we were a little difficult for our mother. It is not unusual for mothers to have a hard time understanding adolescents. Recalling and acknowledging our own contribution to past problems can bring an adult sense of sharing of responsibility for some, if not all, of the wounding events and improve the chances of our being able to achieve reparation with our mother.

As adults, it can still be disappointing and hurtful to realize that our mother is unable to understand our point of view. Our dealings with our mother today echo and rekindle similar feelings to those we had all those years ago as a child. But once we have grown up, we are in an adult-to-adult relationship with our mother, rather than the child-to-parent one of earlier years. In managing our mother today, past hurts should be used as warning lights for areas of our relationship to be changed, rather than emotional triggers to condemn us to suffering the same fate over and over again.

As adults we can more readily grasp our mother's insecurities; this gives us the opportunity to deal better with her. For example, we can tell her how we feel. This still may not be easy for us to do, but it can set in motion a healing process that in the long run will make our relationship with her easier and less stressful.

I recently embarrassed my elder son, Martin, who is now thirty, by being unaware of his feelings. Martin lives just off the Portobello Road, London. In the window of one of the antique shops in the area I had spotted a bucket decorated with a witty painted quotation, and I wanted to go back to the shop to buy it. Martin said, "I'll go with you, Mother—I know the shop owner." In the shop I announced to the owner that I wanted to buy the bucket because I loved the quotation printed on it. When he fetched it from the window for me, I realized I had misread the words and they were not very witty after all. I no longer wanted it.

Embarrassed, I began to do what I always do when I have made a social gaffe: chatter unceasingly. The more I went on, the more uncomfortable my son became. "Mother, come on, let's go," he urged, tugging at my sleeve. "That's enough, Mother. Be quiet!"

I was oblivious to the criticism and my inane chatter continued. Fortunately for me, my son had managed to control his anger (just) and, once outside, he explained to me, clearly and strongly, just how embarrassing I am in such situations. Hearing this, I felt bad that I had embarrassed my son, and realized that I was unaware that I had been doing so. If he had not told me, I certainly would have done it again, and again, unmindful of the impact on him.

Sometimes it will be clear to you that your mother does not understand you. To manage your relationship with your mother you need to acknowledge your role in those painful events from the past, see your mother's actions from her perspective at the time and, as an adult, ask her to be more sensitive to your feelings now.

Pleading for Praise

Bill Goldman survived his teenage years (and the surprise parties at the country club) and grew up to write the enormously successful film *Butch Cassidy and the Sundance Kid*. It opened to rave reviews and full houses. "My wife and I arranged for a special screening in Chicago for my mother to see the movie in style," he explained. "I had a car take her into town, wait for her while she saw the movie, and then bring her home. We called after she was home, and we said, 'What did you think of the movie?' She said, 'The horses were beautiful,' and then she changed the subject. Those are the only words she ever said about the film."

Bill's mother was well aware of his success with this, and other, films. "She was extremely proud of my Oscars. I heard that she would show people my name in the paper—all that stuff. Never told me about it; basically never said anything nice to me about my work."

To give praise seems such a simple thing, and yet it is surprising how often people lament to me that their mother does not do so. Why is this? A complete lack of empathy on her part, because she is either not listening to our needs or too absorbed in her own? Is she afraid her adult children will stop trying hard enough to achieve if they receive praise too readily? Or is she trying to control us by partially withholding praise and therefore love? All these interpretations may contain elements of the truth, but none of them helps us to improve our relationship with her, because they sustain our perceived role as victim.

I have discovered, through working on these questions with my patients, another scenario, perhaps closer to the truth: some mothers do approve of what their children do but assume the children do not have to be told because they already "know" that she is proud of them. The reflected glory of Bill's film successes must have been considerable for his mother. She may well have assumed that he realized this and therefore did not need to hear from her directly how proud she was of him.

Of course, at the root of this thinking is a fallacy that many a mother falls prey to with her adult child: she does not realize that we still want her approval. Our mother is aware just how grown-up we have become, and while she may still like to advise us, she may forget just how emotionally important she remains to her adult children. The truth is that, no matter how old we become, or how outwardly sophisticated and successful, there is a part of us that is always a child at heart, in need of our mother's approval.

Unfortunately, it can feel humiliating to raise this issue with our mother, because as adults we often feel we should be able to get along without her approval. Or we may feel that approval that has to be asked for is not genuine approval. But the fact is that mothers often do approve of us, even if they rarely or never voice that praise. This was the case with Bill's mother. Clearly she was proud of him, and he would have liked her to tell him so. I have seen this issue resolved only by our taking the bull by the horns, and explaining to our mother why we need her approval. It is the sort of issue that rarely resolves itself by our mother realizing for herself that she is failing us. After all, she has probably been doing things this way for many years.

So if your mother withholds praise even when she is proud of you, raise the issue with her. There is a good chance she does not realize she is doing it, or that her approval and praise still count in your life.

Turning the Search for Praise into a Strength

As a bodybuilding champion, Ming Chew has achieved very public success. But he never receives praise from his mother, even though he would very much like to have it. He explained: "My mother went to see two of my shows, out of all of the hundreds of shows I have entered, and luckily I won those two! She is happy that I am successful, but Asians are very stoic; they never talk about the kids' accomplishments. So my mother is not the greatest person for giving compliments. It makes me feel inadequate."

This lack of direct support, coupled with her expectations of high achievement, have caused a lot of tension between Ming and his mother. "I always thought that I had to continue to push, and I think that is a reason why I continue to push today. I have to get the praise that I never got from my mother everywhere else. I realize that is an issue with me."

Ming Chew knows that part of the driving force behind his pattern of hard work is a playing out of his seeking his mother's love and approval from the world at large. The recognition he gets from elsewhere replaces that missing love. But Ming has realized that this compensating behavior is also a strength. There is a hidden advantage to having a mother who expects high achievements but does not praise him for them. "If you are certain of your mother's approval, you don't care about a damn thing. You just say to yourself, 'My mother loves me' and sit back. I think people who accomplish the greatest things probably have the biggest insecurities. And I don't look at that as necessarily a bad thing."

It can be tempting, of course, to try to protect ourselves from a wounding relationship with our mother by rationalizing that a bad situation is in some ways good, and Ming would certainly have preferred his mother to be more praising of his achievements, more expressive in her love for him. But human relationships are complex, and the consequences of certain kinds of mothering are not easily labeled "bad" or "good." More important than such labeling is the fact that once we begin to focus on other, more positive, outcomes of the original events, the negative emotional binding begins to ease a little, and we may be released from our chronic sadness or internalized anger. Ming has to find his support and approval in the world outside his mother, but at least he is not tormented by the poison of resentment. We cannot change our past, but we can change the way we think and feel about it.

Being Ignored

"My mother was consumed with her own interest, which was gambling," Michael Winner declared. "She was not interested in what I was doing. She was really very self-centered." On one of the most significant nights of Michael's life, his bar mitzvah (the Jewish celebration of his passing as an adolescent into the first stage of manhood), she threw a poker party. "I had to sit in the bedroom, which was being used as a cloakroom, a mountain of mink coats all over the bed. I peeped through into the sitting room, and they had put up all these bench tables and were playing cards."

Being ignored by our mother is difficult to bear, because we fear that it means she does not love us. As the psychiatrist M. Scott Peck points out in his book *The Road Less Traveled,* generally when we love something, we want to spend time with it. This is true of even the most mundane aspects of our lives. If we love cooking, then we happily devote many hours in the kitchen, and to buying recipe books, choosing cookware and purchasing the ingredients for our culinary efforts. If we love antiques we devote many hours to finding, buying, restoring, and caring for them. Likewise cars. Or gardens. Or books. And so, Peck says, if mothers love their children, they spend time with them.

But not always, unfortunately. While all mothers have episodes when they are distracted and not attending to their children, some mothers are not interested in their children at all.

Michael learned to cope with being ignored by his mother by becoming self-sufficient from a young age. "I was an only child, so I got on with my own life. I didn't really have a life with my mother. I started writing at the age of four. I formed a life of my own that worked very well."

When he was only fourteen, Michael started writing a show business column in a group of newspapers. As a result he was able to meet the movie and musical stars he had always loved. Sometimes he was able to do so on his own. "I remember once my mother was sitting with a friend, and I went up to her and said proudly, 'Mother, last night I had dinner with Louis Armstrong. Just me and him and his wife.' 'Oh,' she said. 'Wonderful,' she said. 'Louis Armstrong,' she said. Then she turned to her friend and said, 'You know last night, Harold Rose had a two of clubs, Mrs. Beatty had a seven of spades, and I played no trumps . . .' You see what I mean? The interest span in me was . . . well, limited."

In my experience as a psychotherapist, mothers who ignore their children do not intend to hurt them. They love them as best they can, but they are too bound up in themselves and their own concerns to be aware of the needs of others. Michael said, "She was not prepared to give of herself to me as a human being. She treated me as a child-object that she had created. She just wanted to say, 'This is my child and isn't he clever? Look, he's writing articles.' Whereas my father read the articles and took great interest in them."

If our mother is absorbed in her own world, she cannot get to know us and be sensitive to our unique needs. As children, we sense when our mother is not paying attention to us, and we feel rejected.

"Everyone *says* the distancing from my mother damaged me," he confessed, "in the sense that I have never married, so I guess I have never fully trusted women."

I have seen, as a psychotherapist, how a mother's lack of attention to her child can damage that person's ability to connect and be intimate with others. Such people look for others, as adults, to give them the warmth and intimacy they missed from their mother. It is almost impossible for anyone to replace such a deep well of need, and this makes intimate, stable, adult relationships difficult.

Michael believes his mother loved him even though she did not pay attention to him. Some people might think otherwise, considering paying attention an essential requirement for a mother who truly loves her child. But no one mother is all one thing—good or bad, critical or uncritical, supportive or destructive. If we can think about our mother in this way, we can accept her love in the form in which it is offered. If we think there are certain elements that are missing, that does not invalidate our positive feelings toward her, or her feelings toward us. Remember that warming to those elements of our mother we like does not mean we have to approve of the other, more difficult, ones.

Michael's mother is now dead, and he has come to terms with the troublesome aspects of his relationship with her. He spoke warmly of her: "She was a very beguiling person, a woman of immense charisma. Her attitude toward me obviously scarred me, but she had many great qualities." Understanding and acceptance go together. His story reminds us that it is perfectly possible to envisage our mother as lacking in an important dimension, like not paying attention to us, but still loving us and deserving to be loved back.

You're Upset, So Your Mother's Upset

"When I was a child, and I was upset about something," said John Cleese, "my mother was not capable of containing that emotion, of letting me be upset but reassuring me, of just being with me in a calming way, that it was all going to be all right."

John is describing one of the archetypal images of motherhood: a mother rocking her crying baby back and forth in her arms and containing feelings that are too huge, too unknown, too terrifying for the child to deal with. But sometimes a mother cannot do this well, because she too is stressed. The baby's distress adds to her own and is more than she can cope with. We have all seen another image of motherhood: the hassled mother in a supermarket, losing her temper with a crying baby or toddler. Occasional lapses in ability to cope with an upset child are understandable. But there are some mothers who almost never handle their child's emotional agitation well. It sets off something in them they cannot contain, and they become as distressed as the child. This chronic inability to calm us, when we are small, has consequences for us even into adulthood.

"Mother always got in a flap when I got upset, so I not only had my own baby panics and fears and terrors to deal with, but I had to cope with hers, too," John explained. "Eventually I taught myself to remain calm when I was panicked, in order not to upset her. In a way, she had managed to put me in charge of her. At eighteen months old, I was doing the parenting."

In learning to control his emotions at too young an age, John was having to invalidate his own feelings, whereas if our mother contains our panics, just the fact that she is reassuring us confirms that we are understanding the world correctly. If as young children we feel our mother does not acknowledge our distress, we feel alone, trying to cope with emotions that are too powerful for us and which, in a sense, we are not supposed to be experiencing. Instead of gradually becoming familiar with these emotions, and thus learning to cope with them, we have to rely on rigidly controlling them. The aftermath of this can be felt right into adulthood: "The effect has been, I think, that when I was under stress, I found it difficult to ask people for help," John continued. "I always felt I had to handle it on my own by shutting off. That probably increased my sense of isolation and increased the stress."

If, like John, you had to cope by yourself with the turmoil of childhood emotional intensity, it is not surprising that as an adult you feel anxious when emotions surge up that are hard to handle. You may find that you cut yourself off from your feelings and feel uncomfortable when people around you are experiencing anger or sadness. Strong feelings, when you cannot avoid them, make you anxious, so you withdraw from them in a way that can seem cold and uncaring. If you find you are containing your distress rather than asking others for help, it may be a reflection of how your mother behaved toward you when you were young.

Of course, we cannot turn the clock back and ask our mother to do a better job of containing our childhood distress a second time around. But we can recognize what has gone wrong and what the probable implications are for our emotional life as an adult. This may at least prevent us from simply blaming our mother for failing and projecting unarticulated feelings of resentment onto her.

There are many reasons why some mothers find it difficult to contain their child's emotions. In their book *The Mom Factor,* psychologists Henry Cloud and John Townsend suggest several. When a child is upset, expressing anger, fear, or panic, a mother may be overwhelmed by the intensity of the emotions, which so disturbs her that she feels helpless and withdraws from being motherly until her child calms down. A mother who cannot handle her child's feelings may also exaggerate in her mind the seriousness of her child's upset, and overidentify with the child. Because her child is unhappy, her own out-of-control self begins to emerge, and this frightens her. She might punish her child for having "wrong" feelings, saying such things as,

"Stop crying, or I'll give you something to cry about!" She might even be looking for some support and soothing from her child, rather than giving them to her child. Underlying all this may be her feeling that if her child is in distress, she must be failing as a mother, and this makes her anxious to control the child's feelings.

These are some of the difficulties our mother may have experienced in trying to contain our childhood distresses and upsets. Being aware of them helps us to understand why she might not have been able to cope. It does not make us feel better about our original anxiety, and it leaves us still with the problem of overcoming the emotional insecurities we suffer today as a result. But it might help us to see our mother as a victim too, to ease our anger with her, and to open a bridge of communication with her that might have been blocked for a long time.

When Your Mother Doesn't Listen

All mothers are occasionally unable to read our emotional communication, the subtext of what we are saying. But when this is a habitual failing, it engenders a feeling of rejection.

John Cleese recalled such an incident from his days as an undergraduate. During his final examination for his law degree, he was anxious about the last paper, on criminology. But he excitedly rang his mother right after the exam had finished and told her, "I got the questions I wanted on my criminology exam; I knew the answers, so I am sure I have passed, and that means I've got my law degree." There was a long silence, and she said, "You remember those greeny-brown socks that you took back to university at the beginning of the term . . . ?" He remembered "experiencing in that moment a kind of jaw-sagging, breath-taken-away, stunned feeling of resignation, with my excitement just leaking away."

From a very early age, if we do not sense that our mother listens to us we feel she does not really love us. If we are trying to communicate something emotionally important and she breaks into the conversation with more mundane concerns of her own, we feel deeply hurt. Since through childhood we interpret much of what our mother does with us as typical of the whole world, we generalize her lack of interest in us. This is what happened to John. "As a result, I think for many years I was genuinely puzzled when people seemed to be interested in me or in what I was saying," he said.

As a psychotherapist I have worked with adults who had this sort of rejection from their mother, and so are unable to see or accept real love when it is available. They may experience it as suffocating because they never become accustomed to receiving it from their mother. Thinking through this sort of experience with our mother requires that we understand that her lack of response to us was specifically between us and our mother. As adults, we need to free ourselves from the childhood emotional tyranny of thinking that "mother equals everyone else in our life."

The next task is to focus on what exactly was going wrong. If our mother was not listening to us, we naturally interpreted this as meaning, "I am not worthy of interest." In fact her lack of attention was not our fault, but rather a failing on her part. We might assume that a mother would make a special effort to attend closely to what her child is communicating, but sometimes the reverse happens. Because she is involved in all the motherly caretaking roles of cleaning, feeding, and clothing us, she may feel as if she is attending to us, even when it is clear to us that she is not. Further, many people are so wrapped up in their own concerns that they find concentrating on someone's communication difficult.

Are there ways of thinking about this problem which could lead to a more positive perspective? While not proposing that your original interpretation of your experiences with your mother was wrong—it almost certainly captures part of the truth—this book aims to encourage you to consider a range of other interpretations that may also contain an element of the truth and may serve as bridges to understanding your mother better.

When John told his mother about his examination success, he expected that she would understand what he was communicating emotionally—his excitement, relief, and perhaps the hope that she would be proud of him. It was a shock when she failed to register any of this. He understood this to mean that she was not at all interested in his achievement. But it is also possible that, for instance, she simply was not concentrating, and heard his message as a straightforward account of a technical matter concerning his exam. Perhaps she failed to grasp the larger meaning of what he was saying.

Trying to embrace alternative perspectives is made difficult by the fact that we have often lived with our original victim interpretation of the story for years, even decades. And usually we have a fund of other incidents to convince us we were right the first time, so that if someone offers us a different construction we can reply, "Ah, but, she also . . ." and produce another of our stories. Remember that in developing our guiding image of our mother, we tend to remember events in a form that fits with theory. Give yourself time to consider all possible new angles.

John certainly has other experiences with his mother that support the notion that she seldom genuinely cared about him. "I don't think she was capable of loving people except for brief moments, when she was feeling very good. The times when I felt a real concern from her have been very occasional and fleeting." John explained that he therefore rarely used to tell his mother about any problems in his life. "But on one occasion I was talking with her on the phone, and I thought, 'Why protect her?' So I told her that I'd been very depressed for a period of time. Well, she rang me about four days later—and I was slightly surprised because I normally call *her*—and she said, 'I called because I was concerned about you.' And I thanked her, and said, 'Well, that's very nice—I'm touched that you're concerned about me,' and she said, 'Well, of course I'm concerned about you—you're the only person I've got left to worry about me.'"

This sort of encounter is not what we would wish from our mother, naturally. But in thinking through our experience, we need to remember that the mother we have today is not the same woman who was our mother when we were small. We need to ensure that we are responding to the changed woman, rather than to the mother of all those years ago. Today she is a woman who is perhaps maturing; certainly she is aging. It sometimes helps to look for specific ways in which she has changed which might alter your interpretations of her behavior.

John's mother is now very old. A different perspective on her comment, "Of course I'm concerned about you, you're the only person I've got left to worry about me," might be to accept it at face value, as a legitimate anxiety for someone who was ninety-four years old.

John has indeed recognized how his mother has changed, and he has tried to deal as much as possible with his feelings about the woman who is here today, rather than the emotions connected with his internalized mother, the image of his mother he had as a child. "I think I have gone as far as possible in the last few years to loving her," John said. "I would not categorize it as a very strong example of love. But there is a kind of affection, and a kind of acceptance of her. I don't really connect that person who was my childhood mother with the woman I see today. I thank God that she has lived so long, because I think it gave me time to make about as great a degree of reparation with her as is possible, given what happened in the early years."

Making reparation in this way with the mother whom you see as an adult, rather than the mother you remember from childhood, is a good example of what you can achieve in learning how to manage your mother.

Accepting That Your Mother Doesn't Love You

Our mother's love is something that we can never take for granted. Sometimes mothers reject their children from birth, without really knowing why. This rejection can be difficult to overcome. "I was told that she wouldn't touch me for the first six months of my life," said John Goldwyn. Things did not really improve throughout his childhood. He remembered, "One night I had an argument with her at the dinner table, and I looked at her and said, 'From this point forward we just won't talk. That's it.' And I didn't speak to her for about ten years." But eventually he managed to overcome this deep antipathy, and gradually built a warmer relationship with her. To achieve this, John had to accept the fact that his mother had never really been able to accept him in her life. "I know she was indifferent about me," he said. "Before she died, I said, 'I love you very much,' and she replied, 'I respect you.'"

John accomplished a closer relationship with his mother by concentrating hard on what she *could* give him. It was not the warmth and love we all crave, but it was not hostility either, by the end. She did respect him. She even acknowledged her own failings in being a mother to him; on one occasion, she said, "You turned out a great deal better than I ever expected you would, and God knows that was not because of me. I didn't do a very good job."

We can all sense what it must have taken from John to build a relationship of warmth with a mother who did not love him in the way that he, and we, would wish. To recognize that our mother may not ever be able to love us in the way we want is an important step. If we can do this, as John's experience shows, we can take even a meager amount of love and build a workable relationship on it. John's reward for accomplishing this is that his mother appreciated him in the way she knew how.

"I had some good years with my mother," he said. "She and I grew very close."

Rupert Klein had a similar start to John Goldwyn's. "I was never hugged," Rupert said. "Not once. It reminds me of the song from *Oliver*, 'Where Is Love?' Well, I had none of that, and it has affected my life badly in personal relationships. I had no model for them. My emotional education was movies. It still is. I expect all romances either to be terrible ones like Bette Davis romances or wonderful ones like James Stewart romances. I still wait for the background music, and I still expect every encounter or every event in life to have a neat resolution. I expect the show of life to be either a hit or a flop. I'm never prepared for the fact that it's a *sort* of a hit . . . But in my entire education I had no role models at home."

It is an interesting thought that our relationship with our mother provides a sort of model for love relationships—and indeed for relationships in general. For Rupert, there was no clear and grounded love relationship with his mother, and so his model became the simplified and dramatized version of relationships that is depicted in popular entertainment. In fact, this model and the images that create it are very strong for all of us, presented glamorously and attractively in films, books, popular music, and so on. But obviously these exaggerated and entertainingly overwrought stories are not as appropriate as a close relationship with our mother as a model for relating to other people.

If you found your relationship with your mother difficult when you were growing up, you might examine now how your perception of other relationships has been modeled. Did you fall for the fiction of popular drama instead of something more grounded and real? If so, perhaps you should reexamine your model, for it might have led you astray in negotiating the rocky road of adult emotional life.

Bad Mothering Is Misplaced Love

"I was in analysis for about eight years, and God knows I talked a lot about my mother," Rupert Klein confessed. "I'm happy to report that my analyst finally said, 'I have to say, she's the creepiest mother I've ever heard of.'" Rupert had many problems with his mother, but he worked very hard as an adult to overcome them, including undertaking psychotherapy. "I was trying to understand her. It didn't make me like her any more, but I figured the only way you can get along with people you are forced to get along with is to try to understand them." Eventually, his insights into her psyche found their way into his work. "A writer puts himself in other people's heads, minds, and hearts. So I found I could write my mother quite sympathetically. And when I did this, it of course explained everything."

When Rupert's mother read about the women he had based on her, she did not recognize herself. After reading one bestseller she said to Rupert, "Well, believe it or not, there *are* women like that!"

What writing about his mother made clear to Rupert was the root of her hostility toward him: "She didn't want me. Her love was misplaced onto herself. She hated my father, and she hates me. I interfered with her career; she didn't want a baby around the house. Not to mention the deleterious effects on her looks. That's why all those Bette Davis characters don't want to have children!" Rupert's mother's real love was her work. "She was a hard worker, and she was very good at it. She loved working."

If you were a child of a mother who seemed to love her work more than she loved you, you may have felt the way Rupert did. He saw his mother's love as "misplaced," away from her child and onto herself, and as a result Rupert feels he did not get any love from her. But he now feels that he understands the basis of his mother's bad mothering, which helps him cope with her better.

The story of Rupert's mother raises the issue of the difficulties women face in dividing time, energy, attention, loyalty, and even love between their work career and their children. When Rupert was young, it was considered quite outrageous for a woman to prefer her career to her family. With the rise of feminism in the 1970s and 1980s, greater understanding and tolerance is now shown to women who face this dilemma and choose a career. But it is still difficult for mothers to get this balance right. It is an issue there is not the space to explore here, but certainly as a society we should treat it as a priority to offer the right kind of support to working women who become mothers.

If your mother preferred her career to you, and you felt that her love was displaced away from you on to her work, try to understand the emotional dynamics behind that situation and the conflicts of loyalties she experienced as a woman. The pain of rejection will still be there, but it may feel slightly less personal—less a rejection of you and more an inadequate response to her life circumstances.

Dreaming of Love and the Absence of Love

Sometimes our dreams are not about the concerns and characters of our everyday life, but touch deeper layers of our unconscious. "I realize now that I didn't understand how difficult my relationship with my mother was, until I had this dream," said Lauren Hutton. Her dream, recounted here in full, illustrates how powerfully our image of our mother lives inside us.

"In the dream I went to war," she began. "It was in the days of the Vietnam War, and in it I was in my old junior high school. I was fighting through the corridors. It was a very poor southern junior high, and there were all these open poles with a little roofing tar paper to keep you from the rain when you went between the outbuildings. So I was fighting my way from pole to pole and there were Vietcong everywhere, absolutely everywhere, in twos and threes and singly. I was fighting inch by inch toward some place that I didn't know, but I had to get someplace and they were trying to stop me.

"So I fought single-handedly and I killed something like 146 men. It took hours and hours and hours, and by the time I got through all these guys—they were coming from this corner, that side, from under that tree, under that rock and I was ducking and diving and jumping—by the time I got to where I was going I had one arm gone. I was crippled and couldn't walk, but I was crawling and I was shot all over the place—I was a mess. But I was still there.

"So I finally got to where I was going, an ancient door in an old brick building, one of those pre–Civil War buildings from Charleston. It was a brick structure with a giant door like a wine cellar door, and it was half buried in rubble. I only had one arm left and I was digging the rubble away from the door with this arm until my fingernails were all gone; my fingers were a mess.

"The Vietcong were dead and there were bodies all around me. I got all the rubble away from the door, and I was able to push the door and it swung open. And I was looking down into a giant ballroom lit by candle chandeliers, and it was the end of a stately dance, and all the women were in antebellum gowns and the men were all in white tie and long tails, and they were in a line and the men were just bowing. I don't know how, but I knew that this quadrille had been going on for over a hundred years and I had opened the door just at the end of the dance.

"The door swung open, and they started slowly filing out. As they came out, I was lying there because I was crippled and I couldn't get up, and I saw my mother. She was in a white gown, with beautiful magnolias, looking like she did when she was a gorgeous, young fairy-tale princess of a mother. She was coming by and I thought, 'It's my mother! Mommy!' As she came by, her gown brushed over my face and she didn't even look down at me. She just filed past and that was the end of the dream."

Lauren's dream is a vivid example of the "internal mother" we all keep in our unconscious. As a child, Lauren felt unwanted, and the dream reflects the legacy of this into her early adulthood. Since having the dream, she has spent a lot of time and effort in making reparation and establishing rapport with her mother. "I'm still trying, and to some degree I have succeeded," she said.

Dreams can be enormously revealing in dramatizing for us aspects of our life that are beneath our conscious awareness. But dreams come as gifts, not images for us to summon whenever we wish. For many years I wished I could dream about my mother, but I never did. I loved my mother, but I suspect that because she died so young, I was unconsciously furious with her for leaving me, and I could not dream about her.

Then I met John, my husband. I had been with him for about two months when I had a dream in which I was in a car with my mother. We were lost on the interstate, and we could not find the way back. We were arguing. My mother and I did not argue in real life, but in the dream we were really fighting. She finally said, "Pull over into this gas station and ask directions." We drove into the station, and the station attendant was John.

When I thought about this imagery, it seemed to reveal to me that although my mother and I never argued, I really wanted to shout and fight with her, but I could not because she was so ill. I can remember being angry and upset, not necessarily at her, and hiding my face in the pillow so that my mother wouldn't hear me crying because she was so ill. I was very angry and could not let it out.

I was an adolescent when my mother was dying of cancer. That is an age when we need our mother to be there for us in a strong and supportive way. My mother *was* there, but I felt guilty about taking any strength and support from her because she was ill; it was as though I was sucking energy from her. And

I now realize that I always felt that she had not given me enough fuel to get me through life. Then I met John, and when I looked at the dream I realized that perhaps he was there as someone healthy and strong who could refuel me, for I had been depleted for so long.

Interpretations are necessarily personal, of course, but dreams can reconnect us with aspects of our relationship with our mother that we might not otherwise understand.

When Time Heals the Wounds

In thinking through experiences in which we thought our mother did not love us, we can as adults take a view over a longer time span. Our mother may have behaved in certain ways she thought right, but when she matured realized that they may not have been the best for us. Also, when we grow older, we can sometimes see other aspects of our mother, and appreciate that she was not quite as distanced from us as we feared.

"So many memories of my mother are connected with parting," Richard Eyre said. "When my mother took me to boarding school when I was seven, and left me there, I can remember every single detail about that occasion, and it has left a permanent imprint that, try as I might, I cannot erase. It was one of those hot September days in late afternoon, when the light had started to go. There was a big playing field, and a Victorian building with a flagpole outside, and all these very small seven-year-olds. They were either completely white-faced and racked with grief, or very outgoing. I was in the former category and unable to articulate anything. Mother gave me a hug and left me, and as the car pulled away, she turned and waved, and I remember thinking, 'I'm on my own.' It was a terrible feeling. There was a wood with a rookery just by, and I heard the cawing of the rooks, and even today, every single time I hear rooks, I think of that nightmare."

The shock of this abandonment has stayed with Richard all these decades, through his adult life, and at certain times he has felt very angry about it. "I wish I could say there were more moments when I felt close to my mother. That is probably my fault as much as hers, because I always felt she was kind of longing to embrace me. And when I grew up, there were occasions when she made an effort. When I started directing plays, my father never came to see a show of mine, but my mother came to see an early play I did called *Comedians*. It was extremely violent and disturbing, and she responded to the play by seeing it as a kind of scream of pain from me, and a sort of revenge. She said to me, 'I am so sorry you were so unhappy at school,' and I said, 'Well, I was actually.' Of course the pain for her was realizing I had gone through ten years of school and that neither she nor my father had said to me, 'How are you getting along?'

"But I can remember taking my mother to dinner after the play and seeing for the first time, really *seeing,* a woman who is sensitive and intelligent. I realize now that I loved her so much."

Where Mother Love Is Lacking

We have seen that the very primacy of our relationship with our mother means that, as well as closeness, warmth, and pleasure it can also be the source of some of the most disturbing and potentially destructive of emotions. When mother love is lacking we are, as children, vulnerable, damaged, and often alone; and our mother's treatment of us can be painful and wounding. Sadly, there exist mothers whose love for their children is so lacking that these effects are felt to extremes.

Alison Richards had such a mother. Alison, now in her midforties, was an only child. "My mother died about twenty years ago; not soon enough," she said bluntly. "My mother was the devil; she was evil. She was obsessed with sex and religion. I was an abused child. If this had happened today, my mother would have been put in jail."

Occasionally, people experience childhoods that are so seriously devoid of mother love that they provide an example of cruel mothering. If we look at what happens when a mother–child relationship goes as seriously wrong as this, it puts into perspective the more moderate experiences most of us have had. Since Alison's account encapsulates the hallmarks of the worst mothering, it is reported in some detail here.

"I have no problem with talking about it anymore," Alison went on grimly. "Her physical abuse meant broken arms and broken legs. I remember when I was small trying to pick up two glass milk bottles in my grandmother's entry hall, which was marble, and they fell and broke. I remember my mother beating me so hard that I was hitting one wall in the living room, and the only thing that stopped me moving was when I hit the other wall; and I remember rolling like that back and forth. I very often wake up thinking I am falling off the bed, and I dream all the time that she is back. She used to lock me in closets, and to control the panic and pass the time, I would memorize the contents of all the shoeboxes in my closet. I can still tell you exactly how many pairs of shoes I had, what boxes they were in, and what stores they had come from. Also, I would hide chocolate in them to comfort me the next time my mother locked me in the closet. My mother was so emotionally disturbed she had to be put in the hospital for as long as a year at a time."

Alison was relieved when her mother left for the hospital. "But I was terribly guilty, because I wanted her to die. We were Catholic and I was sure God was going to come down and strike me dead for my evil thoughts. And I knew she would eventually come home, because she always did, and when she came home the abuse would always be much worse." She paused for a moment. "My mother was very intelligent," she said, out of the blue. It was the first complimentary remark she had made.

"But I have no fond memories of my mother. When I was little, one of her favorite pastimes was that she'd pretend to telephone St. Joseph's Orphanage, and she'd say into the telephone, 'Today is the day I am going to give her away.' I'd beg her not to give me away. *Beg* her. She'd pack a suitcase for me and put me out in front of the house, and there I was for eight hours, in New Jersey in the hot summer, waiting for the orphanage to come get me. I didn't catch on that it was a game until I was older. I kept waiting to be given away."

When Alison was younger, her mother forcibly gave her enemas. Later, when she was a teenager, the physical and psychological abuse continued. "She would take my favorite clothes and cut them up into pieces. I would come home from school and all my prettiest dresses would be cut and left in a pile, like a haystack in the center of the room. And she would insist on shaving me under my arms. She would make me stand against the bathroom door with my arms up and she'd nick me and she'd cut me, like six times under each arm. And when I got my periods, she said, 'Oh, now you think you are going to be attracting boys? I'll show you.' She marched me into the bathroom and shaved my head from front to back, leaving only the sides long."

Her mother was obsessed with Alison's sexuality and tried to prevent her from expressing any aspect of it. "She'd let me invite friends over, and then she'd come into the living room and say to them, 'I am phoning your parents and telling them the dirty things you have been doing to each other. You didn't think I was watching but I was.' It killed her that I was popular. My mother didn't have a friend in her entire world. Now I have so many wonderful friends; it is a great source of pride for me, because I was never allowed to have any friends. Even so I was popular at school. I just took the looks that I had, and the brains that I had, and I wove myself another life.

"One boyfriend, a star of the football team, came over to see me at our house, but it was a very hot day and he began to suffer from heatstroke. She said, 'Put him in my bedroom and put a cold washcloth on his head to cool him.' I did this, and left him there to recover while I came back in the kitchen to do the dishes with her. It was fine; I never thought about it again. Soon he felt better and got up, and later he left. That night at dinner, my mother turned to my father and said, 'I didn't want to bring this conversation up, it pains me so to bring it up, but I have to tell you, I caught Alison in our bedroom today with her boyfriend.' I said, 'That's not true,' and she said, 'Well, was your boyfriend in our bedroom today?' And I said, 'Well, yes, he was—you sent me in there to put a cold washcloth on his head,' and she said, 'I didn't send you in there, I *caught* you in my bedroom.'" Alison's voice had become tight and choked. She stopped and swallowed hard. "I was always defending myself against my mother."

It seems incredible now that Alison went through this torture for so many years without anyone rescuing her.

"Nobody did anything about it, because in those days it was an embarrassment; no one talked about child abuse," she said. I know the truth of this, because I saw in my years as a consultant to schools that until recently adults were always believed over children. If a child was bruised or had a broken arm and the parent said, "She fell off her bike, she tripped, she's a clumsy girl," the matter was closed. "My father looked the other way, too, I have to say," Alison added. "He didn't know what to do. He loved me madly, but he was terrified of my mother. Lack of intelligence. Lack of balls. When my mother didn't speak to me, which sometimes would go on for six or seven weeks at a time, no one was allowed to speak to me, including my father. I would get locked up as soon as I came home from school and the only friend I had was my dog."

Her mother was particularly fixated on Alison's sexuality in relation to her father. "She was the most worthless human being, always accusing me of making sexual passes at my father. The days that she changed the linens in the house, she would dress me up in them as a bride, and then she'd take out a butcher knife, and say she was going to cut my finger off if I ever touched him."

But once, when she was growing older, her mother went

too far, even for her father. "When I was sixteen years old, I came downstairs in a bathrobe and I was trying to do the laundry—I had to do everything; I was a slave. And I guess the robe had shrunk, as she accused me of coming down in a robe that was too short, to try to attract my father's attention. She was a much bigger woman than I am—she was a good 165 pounds and about five feet nine—and she put her two feet on my feet and punched my face like a punching ball. I tried to turn around to get away from her, and this ankle was so badly wrenched that it damaged the nerves in the foot and I was on crutches for a year. I yelled in pain, 'Stop, it's my foot, it's my foot,' and she said, 'It's not your foot, you lying bitch.' Then my father saw the damage to my foot and, for the first time, he said, 'That's it, you have gone too far,' and he took his fist and he hit her so hard she flew right across the room. When the ambulance came, he said to her, 'If you ever put your hands on her again, I'll throw you out of this house.' And she never touched me again."

Most of us can recall individual incidents when our mother treated us unkindly or even harshly. Usually it was a temporary lapse in our mother's self-control, when she succumbed to her own problems and pressures. In fact, most mothers will admit that they have felt the urge to strike their children at one time or another, especially when a child won't stop crying, nagging, or defying them. This urge can have less to do with the child's behavior than with the mother's own exhaustion, stress level, anxiety, or unhappiness.

I never saw myself as a particularly wonderful mother. When my children were babies I was working full-time trying to make ends meet. My second child had a series of illnesses and cried a lot, and it was very hard for me to tolerate the stress this caused me. I can remember placing him down in his cot, leaving the room and shutting the bedroom door, crawling down the hall, and thinking over and over to myself, "I will not hurt him, I will not hurt him." Most of us resist the impulse to hit our children. Unfortunately, Alison's mother was out of control.

In circumstances as extreme as this, we have to ask the question, Is reparation possible? Did Alison's mother go too far for Alison ever to want to love her? How can anyone who has gone through an experience such as Alison's possibly love their mother, or care if she loves them?

Many years later, Alison's mother lay in the hospital, dying. She suffered from congenital heart disease, and was frequently admitted to the hospital, seriously ill. In adulthood, Alison had moved from New York to California to get away from her mother, but she frequently traveled back to see her in the hospital. "I would go to New York to visit her from California, and if I didn't have a big enough present of a certain value she would have a fit of temper. Anything I had, she always wanted. If I got a fur coat, she'd want one, too. If I got a diamond, she wanted three. On the last visit, I was carrying a Gucci wallet, and she said, 'I want a wallet like that.' I said, 'Fine, I'll give you a wallet like that when you come home from the hospital.' She died while I was on my way home. I was the last person who saw her alive."

Alison's mother had been cruel to her daughter, in childhood and as an adult, yet Alison had continued to fly coast-to-coast to visit her in the hospital and to buy her gifts. Why?

"Because she hated me, and I wanted her to love me," she said.

Alison's story, thankfully beyond the experience of most of us, reminds us just how compelling is the relationship of mother and child. It also suggests that if you feel that your mother hated you, and did not respond to your attempts to build a bridge in your relationship, it is better to acknowledge it openly to yourself, as Alison does, rather than repress it. If you give yourself credit for the efforts you made and address your suffering, you are more likely to make progress in the crucial process of healing your wounds.

Loving Your Mother Is Optional

When I was undertaking psychoanalysis as part of my training, I remember complaining to my analyst, a long time ago, that because my immediate family had died when I was young, I had tried to get closer to my extended family, including cousins, uncles, and aunts. But they had been very cold and even mean to me. I was confused about my feelings toward them. "Well, you don't have to love your family," she said. "What?" I exclaimed. "Could you repeat that, please?" I felt liberated by the notion that loving one's family was not an obligation. We need to understand that loving our mother is an option, not a requirement. Grasping this truth is an important step in relieving the guilt we suffer if we do not love our mother.

But, of course, given the choice, most of us as adults would prefer to be able to love our mother, and be loved by her.

3 DISCOVERING OTHER MOTHERS

I was the only grandchild on
my mother's side of the family, and to say that my
grandmother adored me would be an understate-
ment. Each summer I was sent to stay with my
Aunt Flossie, with whom my grandmother lived.

When Aunt Flossie left for work each morning, she would entrust me, then a five-year-old, with the hiding of our favorite jellied orange slices. I was allowed to eat them during the day, but my grandmother was not to know where they were because she would eat the whole bowl and then not want her meals.

Each morning my grandmother and I would wave goodbye to Aunt Flossie as she went to work, then have our breakfast on the terrace, followed by a game of dominoes. After about twenty minutes of dominoes, she would say, "I think it's time for a little snack," and I would be dispatched to "find" the hidden jellied orange slices. Not difficult, of course, since I'd hidden them myself. And during the course of the day, I would try to ration our eating of the slices, but somehow they were always all gone by the time Aunt Flossie came home from work. Of course, as an adult I now realize that Aunt Flossie knew we would finish the orange slices each day, and the game of hiding them was to make me feel grown-up. She knew how much Grannie adored me, and how important I felt being in charge of the orange slice distribution. It helped Grannie and me have fun during the day. There was so much love involved in this little conspiracy.

This chapter is about "mothering," as distinct from "mothers"; about the kind of love and attention that is motherly but does not come from a mother. This may sound strange, for we naturally assume that mothering must come from mothers. But it became clear from the interviews for this book that the mothering we receive as we grow up is not necessarily exclusively from our mother.

If we had such extra mothering and can become aware of it, and who it came from, it may help us to keep our own mother's influence on us in perspective. We can appreciate what she has provided for us over the years, but also know that we were not entirely dependent on her for our mothering.

But mothering from other women is not always simply a bonus. Where the relationship between mother and child has been poor, mothering from other women can be crucial to our survival and development. In this chapter people talk not only about the importance of the mothering they received from other women, but also how it rescued them from distressing emotional circumstances.

A Grandmother's Role

A loving grandmother can have a deep and lasting emotional influence on us, perhaps as important in some ways as that of our mother. Carla Powell's grandmother, who grew up in a little village in Italy, was a great inspiration to her. "My grandmother was a very special, extraordinary woman. She had been a medical student but never finished her study because, at the age of nineteen, she got married. So she practiced first as a midwife. But then more and more, because there were no doctors in the valley and the only hospital was far away, she effectively became the doctor, too. She even conducted surgery, such as amputating people's legs, and she became like a saint to the peasants. Even when a hospital was built in the area, they would not go to the hospital but wanted to be treated by my grandmother.

"My grandmother was a huge woman, with enormous, big boobs," Carla chuckled. "She would deliver babies and then stay up all night and get drunk with the husbands. My father would have to go to fetch her from the tiny villages, and escort her home.

"One time my grandmother had been delivering twins and then had celebrated so much afterward she was completely pickled. My father went to escort her home, but he had been drinking, too. Eventually, they set off for home, she in her horse and cart, my father on his huge old motorcycle. But he lost her. He got home and then realized that she was no longer with him. She had dropped off to sleep, and as her cart had rounded a big curve, it had slewed across the road into the ditch. She had fallen out of the cart, but by a miracle there was a large heap of cow manure by the side of the road, which the farmers were about to spread on the fields, and she had landed right in the middle of it. The next day, they found her, still fast asleep in the manure! It was a wonderful story she used to tell against herself."

Carla's grandmother passed away peacefully at home, at nearly ninety years of age, with a flask of Chianti beside her, probably having had a tipple before she died. The whole valley went to her funeral. "It was wonderful. The most moving thing was that the people at the funeral were all her babies, delivered by her."

Carla's mother was sad and depressed much of the time, and so Carla could not identify with her as a role model. But she was, and is, inspired by her grandmother's lust for life, her adventurous spirit, her professional skills as midwife and doctor, and her warm, laughing presence.

A grandmother had a much more subtle presence for Alison Richards, whose very difficult upbringing was described in chapter 2. In adult life, Alison is quite a stable person emotionally. I wondered how this stability came about despite such disastrous mothering, and whether it might have had anything to do with her relationship with her grandmother. "My mother's mother was a saint," she said immediately. "I adored her. She died when I was in third grade, but before I started school, when my mother had extended stays in hospital I would stay with my grandmother for long periods."

She recalled details of her grandmother. "She had a black dress for wearing in the house, and a black dress for everything else, but she also had wonderful colored underwear. Her long hair, when she let it down, came to her thighs. I would brush her hair for her, and then she would put it in a chignon. In her top drawer, she used to have black purses, and inside them she'd always keep sticks of Juicy Fruit gum for me."

Alison's memories of her grandmother are so evocative and precious to her that they occasionally flood back without warning. "I remember driving to Connecticut one day with a friend. He took out a piece of Juicy Fruit. As he unwrapped it, I started sobbing in the car, and he couldn't understand why I was crying over a piece of gum. But that smell reminded me of her. I can't even smell Juicy Fruit today without getting hysterical."

Alison's grandmother gave her the kind of loving attention she never received from her mother, and by her little kindnesses and tokens of affection she became Alison's emotional savior. "She was wonderful. You know how when you squeeze a fresh orange and get the residue, the pulp? She used to feed me that in a little crystal dish. I always thought it was a delicacy, like caviar. I didn't realize that people usually threw it away until I was much older. She did lots of things like that for me."

The emotional tenor of Alison's memories of her grand-mother shows just how important a grandmother's affection can be, especially if our own mother did not care about us very much.

The role of grandmother is free from the immediate emotional attachment that mothers have to their children, and as a result their sense of personal responsibility for the child is lighter. Grandmothers are less concerned than mothers are about how a child's behavior reflects on themselves and can center on the child's needs and wants in a more carefree manner. When grandmothers are asked to be primary caretakers and to take responsibility for and spend a lot of time with their grandchildren, the boundaries may become blurred. Under such circumstances, grandmothers often act more like mothers and adopt a more restricting relationship with their children.

When Your Mother Is Your Aunt

It was an aunt who filled the role of mother for Laura Walter. Her own mother did not seem able to take on the re-sponsibilities of motherhood. For a period of nearly four years, from the age of two to five and a half, Laura was "mothered" by her mother's sister, an aunt she called Kiki. It was a relatively short period in Laura's life, but a crucial one. While Laura's mother was at work, Kiki would look after Laura. Kiki's own child was already at school and Laura had Kiki all to herself. "She was the one who gave me actual mothering, and it was the only mothering I ever got."

Laura's mother seemed preoccupied all the time with her own problems, and Laura always knew that she was not emotionally mature enough to be a mother. "I can remember at the age of five, sitting there playing, and seeing my mother coming down the corridor, and thinking, 'My God, she is younger than me. I am going to have to take care of her.'"

Kiki eventually moved away and, soon afterward, with her mother and stepfather drinking heavily and fighting, Laura was effectively looking after her two younger sisters. "I was literally keeping two kids alive. I was in a house with two alcoholics who had come to loathe each other, but were stuck together because of the conventions of the 1950s." Laura's stepfather was cruel to her. "He used to beat me every day. He called me his 'whipping boy.' When I was still small, I kept running away, trying to find Kiki. I would go to people's houses and knock on the door, and say, 'Do you know where Kiki lives?' And then they would call the police, and I would be taken home, and then I was in real trouble."

These were really hard times for Laura, and now, looking back, she realizes just what a wonderful mother Kiki had been to her. "She was able to love kids as individuals," she said. "She made me feel like a full person, rather than just a child. She also expected me to be on my best behavior when I was with her, because she treated me as an adult, but with safe boundaries."

Kiki did not totally replace the missing affection, though, for Laura still craved her mother's love. "I desperately wanted my mother to look at me and see me and love me. But she didn't." But Laura realized how crucial her aunt had been in providing some of that missing mothering. Kiki is still alive, and Laura sees her often. "I see her probably five times more often than I see my mother," she said. "She knows how much she means to me, because I mean the same to her. I think that is the only way love works anyway—I have always thought that. I guess that is how I learned it from Kiki. You love to the equal extent that you get loved."

Today, Laura has befriended a five-year-old boy who needs mothering: "His mother didn't want to be a mother, and he had a baby-sitter ten hours a day, five days a week from the day he was born. She would get these great baby-sitters, good women, and then fire them every six months as soon as she saw her child showing any attachment and bonding to them. Meanwhile she would give this child almost none of her own time, except maybe twenty minutes a day, when it would be real intense."

But from time to time the boy's mother has objected to this friendship, so Laura had to determine a way of positioning herself in relation to his mother.

"I started talking to him about it, saying, 'Listen, you only have one mother. I can never be your mother, and I don't want to be your mother. But your mother, when she is at her best, always wants as many people as possible who will truly love you. And so if she is upset, if she seems to be jealous of us spending time together, just remember that is not your mother's best part. That is your mother's worst part, and she doesn't really feel like that in her heart of hearts. In her heart of hearts she wants you to be happy, and she wants you to be loved by other people.'"

Laura understands both the saving grace of mothering from others, and the primacy of one's own mother. Her statement to her little friend eloquently balances those powerful forces in our early lives.

Other Mothers in the Family

While I was doing my training analysis, my analyst and I realized that although my mother was ill from the time I was aged eleven, and could not look after me fully, I had never been deprived of mothering because I had another "mother" who had been there from my birth. In the South of the United States, where I grew up, the economy was such that even poor white families like us could afford to employ black maids. Henrietta, our maid, worked for us for many years, from before I was born until the day my father died. Her husband dropped her off at our house in the mornings, and my mother drove her home in the evenings. This may sound straightforward, but in those days little towns were informally divided into the two sides of the railway tracks. The black people lived on the "wrong" side of the tracks, and the white families lived in the "better" neighborhoods on the "right" side of the tracks. And for safety, white people were not supposed to be out in the "black" side of the tracks after dark. But my mother loved Henrietta and defied this curfew every evening to make sure Henrietta got home safely.

The three of us did the laundry, the ironing, the baking, and the cleaning. The love, warmth, and laughter that I remember from these long, hot days sometimes sustains me internally even today, many decades later, if I feel cold and unloved. Over and over in my interviews I listened to the same type of story from many people. It was almost like a fairy tale: "Once upon a time, there was a lady who loved me . . . "

So I had two mothers in my home, in addition to my grandmother and Aunt Flossie. In my memory my mother always has first place, but I am deeply grateful now, after all these years, for the extra mothering I received.

No matter how good or poor your relationship is with your mother, it can be very confirming and healing to recall other women who mothered you. You may be surprised by how many mothers you had. Picture them in your mind; recall particular incidents with them; if they are still alive, go and visit them. These women played a very important part in your upbringing and your psychological makeup today.

Roger Greaves's "other mother" was more important to him than his own. In the traditional, colonial setting of India, where he spent his early years, nannies were employed to look after the children, and served almost as surrogate mothers, with the real mother hardly to be seen. "When I was two," said Roger, "we were coming back on the boat from India and I wondered who this beautiful, blond, blue-eyed woman was who was on the boat with me. It was my mother."

The image of a child being brought up by nannies employed to take the place of mothers seems to belong to English upper classes of Victorian outlook in the time of the British Empire. In this society, children would spend their lives with their nanny and visits from their mother would often be stiff and semiformal.

Such a style of upbringing existed even after the days of Empire. The three Hambro brothers, who are today successful investment bankers, were raised in England in the 1950s by a nanny in a formal family atmosphere. "As children we led a very old-English nursery-type existence," said the second brother. Raised by their nanny, they were then shipped off to boarding school at a young age. "I could not believe the fact that my mother and father took me to the train when I was just nine, and sent me off to school. They put me on the train at Victoria station, and I had no idea where I was going. Not only did they not go with me, they had never taken me to show me the place before I got there."

"My homesickness was devoted exclusively to our nanny, and not to our mother," said the first brother.

"Oh Lord, no, not to our mother!" agreed the third.

There had never been any close connection between the boys and their mother, even when they were very small. "I never, ever remember sitting on my mother's knee," said the first brother. "I don't ever remember getting a hug from her, or a kiss."

"No, we didn't have a physical closeness at all, ever," agreed the second brother. "That was learned entirely through our nanny, a much more loving and huge-bosomed lady. She arrived immediately after the war when I was a week old, and stayed with us until she died. I was more fazed emotionally by *her* death, when I was twelve or thirteen and had just gone to Eton, than I was by my mother's death. I was shocked by my mother's death, but I was much more affected emotionally by my nanny's."

The custom of employing such help—and while such old-fashioned nannies may be unusual these days, many families employ au pairs or other sorts of child minders to help—does not necessarily mean that the mothers do not love their children. But in families where there is a more distant relationship with the mother the children can feel unloved by their mother, and therefore form an emotional bond with another person in the household, who may compensate for a lack of love in the mother and play a crucial role in "saving" them from feeling utterly rejected.

Discovering Other Mothers

Sometimes we do not realize there was such a person in our life, for her crucial influence may have come when we were very young. When John Cleese's mother had her ninety-eighth birthday, he, my coauthor Brian Bates, and I went out to dinner with her to celebrate. We were eating in a small village where she had moved with John as a baby to avoid the bombings during World War II. She started regaling us with tales about the wartime "knees-ups," drinking, and good times that she and John's father had occasionally enjoyed during those dark years. I asked her how she had managed to go out at night with a small baby.

"Oh, we always had Lizzie," she said.

"Lizzie, your mother's maid?" John said, clearly puzzled.

"Yes, that's right—she did everything for you as a baby."

"What do you mean?"

"Well, she lived with us. I remember she took you out in the country lanes every day, and you took your first steps with her."

John was fifty-seven years old when he learned this. He had had no idea that Lizzie had lived with them and spent so much time with him as a baby. He had been distant from his mother emotionally as a child, because of her absence with illness, and consequently I had always wondered how he came to have the stable, loving part of himself. Suddenly, unexpectedly, we had discovered where it had come from.

The lesson of John's experience is that it is worth our while to think back and make inquiries to try to identify any significant other women in our early life.

Jamie Crawford's mother did not like her. "When she was there she was angry," she said. "I have a memory of her screaming and yelling at me in the library. I don't remember what it was about, but I couldn't have been more than four years old. We did not do anything together; we didn't garden or cook or take walks." Also, Jamie's mother was absent much of the time. "She left, I've been told, when I was about three, to go to Washington, and she really didn't come back until I was about eight."

This was effectively five years without a mother at home. "I guess I was raised by Cecil, my father's butler," she said thoughtfully. "Cecil was my mother. I still love him."

It was the butler who'd done it! I have known Jamie for a number of years, but I had never heard her mention Cecil before.

"I don't talk about him," she admitted. "I guess I haven't been appreciative enough of Cecil for saving my life," she agreed. "Although we do talk sometimes. He's eighty-eight years old now."

Today Jamie realizes more clearly what Cecil meant to her as a child, when she had no mother love. She visits him, and the opportunity is still there for her to express her gratitude and her love for the butler who "saved her."

We all need to think about our childhood and appreciate those people who reached out to us emotionally and gave us love, even if we were in a loving family already.

If you leave it too long to discover your other mothers, it may be too late. Penny Castle's mother was so difficult that Penny, her father, and her two sisters were in a family counseling group because the youngest sister was in crisis. "Finally, we decided to bring my mother in, because the therapy wasn't really right without her," Penny explained. "So she came in and started talking right away about how we needed to be really honest, and cut to the quick, and talk about Annie being with abusive boyfriends, and work out where the abuse started. And then she said, 'Well, the girls will tell you, I never laid a hand on them, ever.' And yet she had regularly beaten us, just for no reason, you know, and sometimes for . . . "

Penny's voice trailed off in painful reminiscence. She can remember having bruises, and a cast to mend broken bones. "When Mother said she had never laid a hand on us, we all stood there, stunned. And the physical scars were the least of it—do you know what I mean? I was the only one who said anything. The therapist said, 'So, does anyone want to respond?' The therapist knew plenty about her and was armed and ready—he'd heard from all four sources." Penny got up and confronted her mother. "How can you say that?" she shouted. "It's just not true!"

But at this point Penny realized something awful, something she had not quite understood up until that moment. "I could see in her eyes for the first time that she really didn't understand. She really had to believe, for her own survival, that nothing had ever happened. It was so clear to me that in that moment I despised her and also completely forgave her. And realized the hopelessness of the whole situation. I knew that we could never rectify it." The certainty that her mother was so strongly in denial shocked Penny, but shifted the blame from her mother to some sort of pathology, some sort of condition that drove her mother to violence and then took away her awareness that she was hurting her children.

Fortunately, Penny's mother had realized that her children were too much for her, and had hired a housekeeper. The presence of the housekeeper turned out to be crucial for Penny and her sisters. Nanny filled a central space in their lives; looked after them, fed them, cared for them. Loved them. But it was not until many years later that Penny was able to appreciate just how important Nanny had been to her and her sisters.

"When Nanny, who had been our housekeeper for nineteen years, died, I went to her funeral. My sisters and I went to this tiny Baptist church in Harlem, with only eleven people attending—people we'd heard about all our lives. It was then that we knew who had saved us. And basically, we mourned the loss of our mother. It was just the most shocking thing. We realized who had really cared. It was something that had never even occurred to me. I really didn't want Nanny to die. Just knowing that she was alive, somewhere in the South Bronx, in an apartment that she'd never let me visit, was just . . . it meant I had some sort of maternal love."

Realizing just what her nanny had meant to Penny is brought home by the intimacy of her memories—the sort of memories that most people have of their mother. "I can still recall Nanny's smell—this kind of salty skin. And when I smell Ben-Gay medicated cream, I think of her, because she used to give me little Ben-Gay rubs when my legs ached from tiredness. I know how she felt—her soft skin and cheeks, her arms and breasts. But not my mother. I saw her recently at a funeral, embraced her and thought, 'What a weird aroma! Who is this person?' And yet Mother was ever present; it's not like she left us. She was there all day, all night."

Physically present but psychologically absent. Well, not absent so much as hostile and malevolent, without realizing she was being so. Penny's "mother love" came from her nanny. She just wishes that she had realized it in time to thank her.

Someone who did realize in time was Bill Goldman. Even so, it was not until he was thirty, and began to see a psychotherapist, that he appreciated just how important a role Minnie, the family maid, had played in his life. At his first session he began to tell his therapist about the main people who had been part of his family. "Whenever I mentioned Minnie's name I would start to cry. My eyes would fill with tears, my throat would get choked and I would start to cry. I was rocked. It went on like that for weeks. Whenever I mentioned her, this terrible drying of the throat, and tears. I kept thinking, 'What is that about?'" Fortunately, the therapy gave him the opportunity to think through his early life, and Minnie's significance for him became clear.

For as long as he could remember, Bill's mother had been totally deaf. "Sometime after the age of ten," he said, "I screwed up the courage to ask her how she had become deaf, and she said four words that echoed forever in my brain: 'When you were born.' Ever since that time, I felt that my mother's deafness was my fault because of the problems she had at my birth. My father became a hopeless alcoholic who eventually committed suicide, which of course I felt was really my fault, too. I found his body."

Bill's family was fraught with tensions, and he felt emotionally isolated as well as having strong feelings of guilt toward each parent.

"But I was one of those people who was saved by the maid," he said. "We had a Norwegian maid named Minnie when I was growing up. In my early years and all through my crucial stages of development, she was the only one who I had any belief in."

Minnie cared about Bill, and was more aware of his emotional needs than were his mother and father. An example of her care was when he was moved up a year at school. "I was the smartest kid in the sixth grade, and they did something that I just hated: They made me skip a grade. It is not an uncommon thing now, but in the Midwest in the early forties it was unheard of. It was freak-like. Minnie came back, and I said, 'Oh, I'm skipping a grade,' and she said, 'That's terrible! You'll lose one year of childhood.'" She knew immediately the emotional price Bill would pay.

Some years later, twenty-five and living with his brother in New York, Bill published his first novel. "The book proofs came and the publishers asked me for a dedication. I remember I said to my brother, 'I'm going to dedicate it to Minnie,' and he said, 'You can't, you'll kill Mother, you can't do it, she'll be humiliated, blah, blah, blah.' And I succumbed and dedicated the first book to my mother, and my second novel to Minnie. *She* was the seminal figure for me; she was the Good Mother, the mother who cared. We were never affectionate and we were never emotional with each other; she was not huggy. She was just very quiet, and had a lot of common sense."

And Bill loved her.

"But because Minnie and I were never very verbal, I

never said to Minnie that I loved her till the end. At first I felt so guilty because I couldn't tell her. I loved Minnie more than anything on earth and I could never tell her that. I have memories as a boy wandering in the kitchen, just sitting there watching her cook, and just being there in that warmth. And of course I felt so guilty about it because it was a forbidden love, a love that dare not speak its name. I loved the maid."

Bill eventually did tell Minnie he loved her and kept in touch with her throughout his adult life. "She stayed with my mother for forty years or more, and then when she was very old, she retired and went up to Minnesota to live. I would call her three or four times a year, and send her a Christmas present. My wife Eileen and I lived in a big duplex in New York, and one night I was downstairs and Eileen was upstairs. I was watching sports and having some wine, and you know that thing when you see something out of the corner of your eye and you look and it's gone? Well, I saw something out of the corner of my eye, and when I looked, Minnie was *there*.

"I went running upstairs and I said, 'Eileen, Minnie was just in the television room. She was standing there and she was wearing her apron and nodding and smiling.' The next day the phone rang. It was Minnie's nephew in Minnesota saying that she had died at that exact same time the previous night. I instantly became a believer in all of this out-of-body stuff. She came to say good-bye."

Today, Minnie's memory remains just as precious for Bill. "I just had my sixty-fifth birthday. I took some friends to the Four Seasons restaurant and I said, 'I want to remember two people who are not here. One of them is Susanna, my daughter, who is in Puerto Rico. The other is Minnie, who is now dead.'"

Bill has noticed how others have had similar experiences. "When I meet people, it's amazing how many were 'saved by the maid.' I must know half a dozen successful men who had the same experience, very often in the South with black mammies who basically ran things. They were the source of affection. Well, Minnie was the source of all affection for me because nobody else gave a damn and I felt so terrible about it. I still do."

A Source of Strength

As a psychotherapist, I have seen many times a loneliness in the hearts of people unloved by their mother, which they seem to carry all their life. It is difficult to put into words what they lack, but perhaps it is the continuing presence inside them of a caring mother, a place where she always dwells, whether she is alive or dead. I am fortunate in that I had a mother who gave me this gift. My mother always presides over me. When things are difficult, she enters quietly into my mind, like a shadow of herself.

I remember vividly such an occasion, shortly after I had moved from America to London. I was struggling with a new country, two young boys, a new job, and a challenging training in psychoanalysis.

One morning I was walking through Regent's Park on my way to work. I had just finished reading *The Magus* by John Fowles. At the end of the novel, the heroine Alison enters this same park and sees a Greek relief. I was looking around to see if I could spot it. And as my eyes found it, to my surprise I began to weep, as I remembered two simple lines of poetry my mother had taught me when I was very small:

> God's in his heaven—
> All's right with the world.

I was so overwhelmed that I sought a park bench to collect myself. What on earth was the matter with me? *The Magus,* at least to me, is about the search for meaning and love in life. I found myself thinking how terribly lonely and difficult my life had been during those initial months in England. And I suddenly realized that my mother, that continuing presence inside me, was looking after and protecting me.

If children are not given love and affection, they have an emotional vacuum that needs to be filled by those precious figures who give them love in their lives: nannies, aunts, maids, grandmothers, friends' mothers, even butlers. And those of us who did feel loved by our mothers had other mothers in our lives too. Our need might not have been so sharply felt as those who were distant from their mother, but these women helped to fill that dimension in our lives that burns warm and comforting inside, like a campfire.

If you can think back and identify who those people were for you, it will help you to understand where your inner strengths come from. If it is not too late, you may be able to thank your other mothers for their love. And if as a child you had to search for mother love outside your relationship with your mother, you need to know this: It's not your fault.

4

A MOTHER'S DREAMS

Many mothers have unfulfilled dreams and ambitions, which remain secret, barely whispered even in their own minds: things they have always wanted to do but have had to set aside in order to attend to the responsibilities of being a mother. We are so used to seeing our mothers in their parental role that we often forget that they could have had another life, and that they have sacrificed aspirations to bring us up. Perhaps they never complain, and so we never know.

There are also mothers who never stop complaining about their unfulfilled dreams. They are "martyr mothers," determined that we should not ever forget the sacrifices they made on our behalf. The price they try to exact is our eternal guilt and undying gratitude. Exploring these two extremes of sacrifice and guilt reveals some insights that may be helpful in understanding our relationship with our mother.

Let us begin with the story of the gold shoes.

Mothers Making Unsung Sacrifices

Carla Santos Shamberg's mother was a second-generation German Lutheran immigrant to New York. Like many of her generation, she dressed conservatively, as was proper for a wife and mother several decades ago in her home culture. All her life she wore simple clothes and plain brown, low-heeled shoes. When she died, Carla went to her mother's apartment to sort out and pack up her personal belongings. "I went through her shoe closet," Carla said. "She had saved, in case she ever needed to wear them again, what seemed like five hundred pairs of worn-out brown pumps. The shoes were all the same— brown pumps with the heels worn down."

But when Carla cleared them away she found, hidden at the back of the wardrobe, a shoebox. Opening it, she discovered a beautiful pair of gold-colored, high-heeled evening shoes. They had never been worn. Gazing at these elegant gold shoes, Carla realized that they represented her mother's hopes, dreams, and aspirations, through many years of honest, plain living as a mother. "They had little fake jewels on them. They had just sat in that box all that time. I thought that was the saddest thing I've ever known. She had a hard life, and I think she was very disappointed not to have been able to do more with it."

Carla's discovery of the gold shoes revealed a hidden side to her mother. She was a woman who had lived a life serving her family but who had secretly yearned for something more; instead of achieving that, she had committed her energy to her children. "She was not a well-educated woman, but she really made sure we got an education and were exposed to more culture than she had ever had. She was always taking us to museums, and she was very interested in our schools. She was a member of the Parent-Teacher Association, and when we went on school trips she would volunteer to go with us. She was a very involved parent."

So what does Carla's story tell us about the sacrifice of being a mother? It encapsulates one of the most important lessons in understanding a mother. The gold shoes symbolize feminine elegance, glamour, allure, romance, parties, dancing, and style, but none of these words is usually associated with being a mother. Mothering evokes qualities such as warmth, patience, nurturing, caring, and mentoring, but we need to remember that these qualities can never define the whole of a woman's psyche. Becoming a mother can entail giving up some dreams in order to deal with the pressing issues of raising children—such as struggling with financial hardship and not complaining about it.

A mother's capacity to hold things together financially when the burden is hers is something that is easy for us to take for granted, especially if she does not complain much. Ming Chew described the story of his mother, and his dawning realization of the sacrifices she had made for him.

His mother had a hard life from the start. As a girl, she worked in the rice fields in China, which was a grueling job, and she developed an eye complaint because of the constant exposure to the sun. After the Communist revolution, Ming's mother went to Hong Kong and entered into a prearranged marriage with Ming's father. He emigrated to America, and eventually brought her over to join him. Because Ming's father was away a lot as a merchant marine, Ming was brought up largely by his mother alone.

When he was growing up and trying to find his identity as a Chinese-American, Ming could not appreciate his mother's difficulty in integrating into a new culture, even though she was trying. He recounted the time when she was preparing for her examination to become an American citizen. "She was going to be asked about the presidents, and how many states there are—all these very basic questions you have to answer to become an American citizen," he explained. "I remember sitting down and grilling her, and I would get so angry because she couldn't get it straight, and she would pronounce all the words wrong. She barely spoke the language. I used to think she was a pain in the ass!" he admitted.

However, when he went to college Ming's attitude toward his mother began to change, and he was able to see her in a different perspective. Because his father had been away at sea for long periods, his mother had taken on the responsibility of supporting them financially. "My mother was a seamstress, and for years she worked in one of those dreaded sweatshops making about two bucks an hour. She worked really hard, five or six days a week, and earned very little money. I didn't know at the time how poor we were, but when I went to college (she always stressed the importance of education, and that was good), I started comparing myself to others. And I realized that we didn't have any money compared with these people." It made Ming think about his mother's life. She had "worked and worked, and saved and saved, and she had got the house for us. I applaud her for that now."

Ming's mother must have been very uncomplaining to have worked so hard for so little, over such a long time, and for him not to realize it. If his mother dreamed of an easier life, a freer existence, she did not make him feel guilty for her sacrifices.

Not complaining can be difficult. I certainly understood the life Ming was depicting, and the way his mother kept the struggle from him. I came from a very poor family, and yet I never knew that we were poor because my parents never said, "Oh, you can't do that, we don't have the money."

One of the most vivid memories I have of my mother was the time I wanted a bicycle, and I wanted a new one. She said to me, "Why would you want a new one when this used one is perfectly okay?" The way she said it made it sound so sensible to buy the used one. It was a much more positive approach than the one I used with my children. I wanted to kick myself every time I heard myself say, "Oh, you can't have that because we can't afford it." My words encouraged a negative outlook. I also realize now that they stemmed from my need to make my children aware of the struggles I was going through to support them. I felt I could draw strength from their acknowledgment of the sacrifices I was making, and my harping on about our poverty relieved my guilty feelings about not being able to provide them with everything they wanted. My own mother, on the other hand, had the strength to resist the temptation to appeal for sympathy in this way, and I admire her for it.

There is an important generational difference here. I grew up in small-town America in the 1950s and 1960s, and I remember when I mentioned I wanted to become a doctor, everyone said, "Oh, you don't want to be a doctor, honey, you just get your teaching certificate, 'cause you'll be married, and you'll need to have a profession that you can work the children around." Today, opportunites for women are better, but many of our mothers grew up in a different era. Then, the expectations were that ambitious dreams were not allowed, and young women would devote their energies to being a mother and a housewife, and fit any notions of work around those primary duties.

In an earlier generation, when it was an accepted norm that women would stay at home and look after their family, it was arguably easier not to be resentful of these demands. And these accounts of sacrifice are not intended to suggest that selfless devotion is the biological and spiritual destiny of every woman who has a child. The point is that we need to know and to respect what our mother gave up for us. In doing so we can recognize that the times are changing: more freedom of choice for women is an important feature of today's expectations. Nevertheless, mothers today, who have not had to give up as much as the generation before them, still have to cope with extra pressures to accommodate their family responsibilities; they cannot usually do everything they would wish outside the home.

The fact is that giving up part of her dreams in order to raise her children is a sacrifice every mother makes, and recognizing this can help us to deal with some of those aspects of our mother that we find difficult, exasperating, and upsetting.

I was reminded of this sacrifice some years ago, when I was working at a school in London. I taught with a Polish woman named Maria. She lived with her mother, and each day at work she would regale me in the staff room with horrendous but hilarious stories of their fraught relationship.

But one day she came into school and seemed very quiet and thoughtful. I asked her if she was feeling all right, and she told me that the previous evening, she and her mother had been reminiscing about their lives, and the conversation had brought back some significant memories. She explained that she had grown up in Poland and when, in September 1939, Hitler's armies invaded, her mother realized that for the sake of her daughter's future, they would have to leave the country quickly. But she had no money, and so to raise the means to help her daughter escape, Maria's mother sold the gold fillings in her teeth. They had to be painfully drilled out.

After Maria had told me what her mother did to rescue her, we both fell silent. Suddenly I saw this difficult woman in a completely different light. I'm not so sure that I laughed so hard at the funny stories after that.

This is an extreme case of personal sacrifice in very difficult times. But in similar ways all our mothers make many smaller sacrifices. While we should not feel guilty for her sacrifice, for she chose to make it, neither should we take such sacrifices for granted. Occasionally turning our thoughts to the hundreds of small sacrifices she made on our behalf—emotional or material—may help us to achieve a more conciliatory perspective, to take a step toward a closer relationship.

The Mother as Martyr

Unless, of course, she continually *tells* you about her sacrifices on your behalf.

For some of us, Mother had it hard, and boy, did she let us know it! It is difficult for us as children to carry the burden of a mother who complains about her struggles, but for many people, the agony drags on into their adulthood. Such a mother is constantly reminding us of the sacrifices she made, the trials she had to overcome, the struggles to make ends meet, the problems we gave her. Her litany of complaints can become a debilitating drip feed of guilt-inducing martyrdom. We are made to feel bad for not repeatedly thanking her for everything, for not being more cooperative after all she's done for us, for not heeding her problems, and for not realizing that because we are ungrateful we are not really worthy children. "You'll appreciate me when I'm dead," she says.

"It was awful," groaned Mike Nichols, recalling his childhood with a mother who suffered from chronic illness. "I remember I had to be quiet when I got home from school; that was the main thing. 'Be quiet—your mother doesn't feel well. Don't make any noise.' When we were allowed in to see her, she was always on the phone at her big table with lots of pills on it.

Illness changed her from a beauty to a stereotypical Jewish mother somewhere along the line, and she kept after my brother and me so much because she wanted to make us feel guilty. We were blamed for everything. She had a series of boyfriends who were also blamed, but we were the main targets. But worst of all, it wasn't that we made her angry, which we could have handled. We 'hurt her feelings.' She was always hurt, always weeping, always upset because we'd done or said something bad. She was a master of guilt. She really was good at it. And it's awful to feel guilty as a kid. I was desperate to get out of there."

Guilt is about responsibility and regret: responsibility for actions that have hurt someone else, and regret because the action cannot be undone. The employment of guilt by our mother to control us involves, as with Mike's mother, the continual ascription to us of blame for things that we are alleged to have done to her, or for which we should feel direct responsibility. Coupled with that, she ensures that we know just how deeply she has been hurt by the action we have taken, or the things we have not done when we should have. In being made to feel blameworthy, we are made aware of how damaging we have been. We suffer from a perpetual sense of being in debt to our mother, under moral pressure to make amends for all the hurts we have caused her. It is a deeply disempowering process, for we are made to feel, over and over again, that we are unfeeling, insensitive, cruel, and unworthy.

It is relatively easy for a mother to control her young children through this martyr mentality, for as children we are still unsure of boundaries and of what we can reasonably be expected to be responsible for. Such mothers are making us primarily responsible for them. As a result, we often feel that things were our fault when, in fact, they were not.

Even when we are grown-up, a martyr mother can still be difficult to deal with. Guilt is a potent weapon against adult children too, for we can easily feel that we are not loving our mother as we ought, or at least not expressing that love in the thoughtful way we should be. "Hello, Michael. This is your mother. Remember me?" is a famous line from one of the celebrated sketches Mike Nichols performed with Elaine May in the 1960s. It is an actual line of his mother's. The rest of us might have more difficulty finding humor in a painful relationship with a martyr mother.

Resisting unfair blaming for things we have done—or not done—can be exhausting, and alienates us from our mother, making us feel even more guilty for not loving her. At the heart of it, these mothers are trying to force us to love them out of a sense of obligation to them. The syndrome can result in years of emotional discomfort through childhood and a chronic fight to feel worthy as an adult.

How do we deal with this? As in so many other aspects of managing our mother, we can gain a foothold on sanity by understanding our mother's point of view. To do so does not mean that we are sanctioning her behavior, but it is helpful for us to know where she is coming from psychologically. One thing is for sure: her behavior does not come from a happy, healthy, and stable emotional state. Rather, the mother who behaves like a martyr is acting out her own problems.

The main feature of our mother's martyrdom is that she finds it difficult to accept responsibility for her own actions and blames us for them instead. M. Scott Peck, in his book *The*

Road Less Traveled, considers this ascription of blame to others, when it is a chronic tendency, to be a character disorder. In not accepting responsibility for her own impact on the world, this sort of mother says things like "I had to," as if she was a person who has no power of choice, whose behavior is completely directed by external forces totally beyond her control. From this perspective, she talks as if all the difficult things she did for us as a mother were done not out of free will and love for us, but because we burdened her with the necessity to do those things. Phrases such as "I worked so hard for you" become accusatory, as in, "If it hadn't been for looking after you I could have done such-and-such." Every mother feels such emotions from time to time, but some mothers think and talk this way most of the time.

But there is another side to the story. "My mother was always announced by her husbands, and her friends, and herself of course, as having had a terrible life," Mike Nichols recalled. "And in a way I guess she did. My mother adored her parents, and lost them as a very young girl. Then she had a difficult time being raised by 'evil' relatives, and made into a sort of stepchild." Her early difficulties were compounded when, as an adult, she left Germany to live in America and then her husband, Mike's father, died. Little wonder that she was left feeling abandoned and devoid of love and support. Her suffering was real enough.

Considering if her response to her personal disasters had been totally negative or whether she had managed to show some more laudable aspects of herself was a different sort of question than the ones Mike was used to asking himself about his mother.

"I'm usually so angry at her that I forget the good part," he said, thinking back to the drastic situation his mother had faced after her husband's death. "And there *was* a good part. She was left with two children, no money, in a new country where she didn't know the language. She went from that to sending us both to good colleges." This is beginning to sound more like the "gold shoes mother" than "martyr mother"; here is a scenario in which his mother's sacrifices could actually be appreciated. "On her own, she got it done," Mike continued. "She worked in bakeries, and as a baby-sitter, then for some shrink as a receptionist, in a bookshop, and then eventually she worked up to being able to start leasing hotels in the Catskills and running them, and supporting us that way. She even had a gift shop in our apartment. She did everything she could think of, somehow scrimping and managing. What she did was an amazing thing."

As Mike talked about what his mother had suffered and achieved, a whole new perspective on her began to emerge. He felt able to acknowledge her achievements and recognized the extent to which he had forgotten this side of his mother's life. "My brother remembers much more than I do. We were unbelievably poor for a long time—so poor that for a while she did seem to give up and we weren't even clean anymore. He has memories of cockroaches and . . . but I've blocked the bad stuff. I have blocked from my memory the positive things she did, too, and I don't really remember a moment of that, either."

So Mike's mother did go through a lot in trying to make ends meet in New York after her husband died, and she succeeded through hard work and determination. The problem was that she never let her boys forget about it, constantly accusing them of not appreciating what she had done, and blaming them for everything that went wrong. But on reflection, Mike is able to understand better his mother's difficult journey through life. This does not directly relieve his childhood hurt, the chronic blaming, the guilt, and the struggle to maintain a relationship as an adult with a mother who was continually attacking him as a way of begging for appreciation, but it is helpful for him.

It is helpful to realize that because children do not usually fully appreciate adult sacrifices on their behalf, it is not surprising that some mothers are tempted to complain about the struggle they are having in order to attract some attention, approval, and support. As adults we know how much recognition of our efforts can make us feel good and strengthen us when we are struggling. A natural desire for recognition does not *excuse* mothers who go too far and become martyr mothers who make us feel guilty for their efforts, but it helps us understand them.

In looking at the way in which mothers make sacrifices on our behalf, we are making a virtue of mothers who do not complain, and branding the mothers who complain to excess as martyrs. Complaining does seem to be a major discriminating factor in people's assessments of their mothers as "good" and "bad." However, we should be aware that stoicism is one thing and repression another. Is the locking away of a natural reaction, the denial of release, a price our mothers *have* to pay? Making one's feelings known about the difficulties of being a mother is a matter of degree rather than absolutes. We would not want to see a hitherto stoical mother turn into a martyr, but it might benefit us and her if we could find ways to help her to release, to let go of emotion she has had to repress during her lifetime of being a mother.

Understanding our mother's vulnerability is one way of starting to liberate ourselves from the tyranny of negative childhood experiences. For one thing, it casts our mother in the role of victim too. And it is possible that the misery she visited on us was not because she was evil, but because she was (and perhaps still is) suffering herself.

To forgive your mother can be a big step, not to be undertaken lightly. To forgive does not mean that you absolve your mother of responsibility for her actions or deny your own feelings about what happened. But understanding why she behaved as she did is a necessary move toward healthy forgiving, in which you know why you are letting go of resentment and blame.

Ultimately, a martyr mother desperately needs love. It is because she needs to squeeze every drop of positive emotion from us that she feels it is essential to make us feel exaggerated gratitude for everything she has done. Her behavior makes us angry as adults, and we feel we want to be more distant from her, to put some safe space between us and the torment of her constant whining. This becomes a vicious circle, because it feels to her as if we love her less (which perhaps we do), and she becomes ever more desperate for us to appreciate her efforts. But understanding her desperate need for recognition and for love will help us to resolve our troubled relationship with this kind of mother.

A Mother Needs Love

There are many games mothers play to gain our attention and our love. Being "ill" is one of the most endemic. When

Stephen Sondheim's mother attempted to do this, she sometimes got caught. "One day she shows up at my house in New York. I open the door and it's my mother. I say, 'Mom, what are you doing here?'

"She takes out a little pad and pencil and writes, 'Can't talk.'

"'Why not?'

"She writes, 'Doctors won't let me.'

"'What's wrong?'

"She writes, 'They don't know.'

"I say, 'Oh, I'm terribly sorry.'

"Really I know it's a load of horseshit but I play along. So eventually she leaves. That day Julie Andrews and Blake Edwards are giving a cocktail party, and they happen to live in the same building as my mother. I go to the cocktail party and as I'm just leaving I think, 'Well, she's upstairs, why don't I call her?' I telephone her apartment. She answers, 'Hello!' in a big, strong voice.

"'It's Steve.'

"'Oh, hi, darling,' she says, in a faint whisper. 'How are you?' So I go upstairs to visit her and she carries on with the whole charade of whispering as though she had not bellowed 'Hello!'"

Clearly his mother was playing the "life is a constant struggle for me" game, fueled by her chronic "illnesses." When our mother loses control of us because we have become adult, she sometimes feels unable to ask openly for attention, because she senses that it is inappropriate now that we have lives independent of hers. But she still craves the kind of attention she used to be able to command when we were younger, and she thinks if she feigns an illness or some other emergency, her child will pay attention to her, and she can regain some semblance of control over the relationship. Naturally we become tired of this game, and pay less attention to her cries of help because we think they are not genuine. The problem, as we all know, is that she is crying "wolf," and so when the wolf is really at the door she may not get the help she needs from us.

Perhaps we need to listen to our mother's complaints in a different way. We may have become accustomed to minimizing the importance of her "symptoms" of illness, or her various "crises" that need our immediate attention. But what we should really attend to is the cry for love that underlies these charades. If we still love our mother, despite her making our life miserable and rendering herself difficult to get along with, we may be able to do something about it. Telling her we love her, if we do, could be the best medicine for her various "ailments" and, most important, might persuade her to let up on the complaining.

Unfortunately, for many of us, telling our mother we love her can be something of a trial. I was a guest last year at a dinner for Rosh Hashanah, the Jewish New Year holiday. My place was next to the host and we fell into conversation about mothers. He told me of a recent dream he had had in which his mother was very ill and dying, and he was very upset in the dream because he had never told her he loved her. He tried to revive her so that he could tell her, but was unable to do so. He awoke terrified, as the dream seemed so real. "It was such a horrible thing that it woke me up, and I was crying," he said.

Struck by the effect this revelation must have had on him, I assumed that he had followed up the message of the dream. "So of course you rang your mother immediately to tell her you loved her?" I asked. A look of utter horror came over his face. "Oh no, you don't understand my mother," he said. "I couldn't do that. I couldn't tell her I love her!"

Why is it so difficult for us to tell someone we love them? Fear of rejection? Of a sneer of indignation that one could be so soppy? Of laughter at such a childish expression? Of exposing a sign of weakness? Or perhaps it is difficult because it strays into an emotional arena which men, in particular, try to avoid.

Richard Martin admitted he does not openly express love toward his mother. "My father, who's a very unemotional man, mocks such sentiment, and says, 'We're not one of those slushy, huggy, kissy families,'" he explained. Yet Richard is generally an expressive person, warm and tactile. The contrast puzzles Richard's wife. "Nobody touches in your family," she says; "nobody says 'I love you,' so how can you be this sensitive person when your family is so very intellectual?" "I think maybe it's a reaction," he replied.

An emotionally closed family might well lead to lack of love expression with our mother, as Richard's example shows, but we can transcend this restricting convention in our lives generally.

As our mother grows older, we know that the time we are going to have with her becomes shorter, and sometimes this helps to overcome the problem of expressing love. Mike Pierce's mother has recently gone through an operation, a serious enough experience to alter Mike's attitude: "The operation has really softened me toward my mother," he said. "But it is hard to display emotion because we have just never done it." Mike wishes that he could express his feelings for his mother more openly. "It's the tough façade. But it is not a strength; it is very much a weakness, because if you can't tell your mother that you love her . . ."

It seems to be much less of a barrier when we are small, but as we grow up the door to tender communication begins to close. "I remember when I became too old to kiss my mother good night. I was like, 'I am a big guy now—I shouldn't be doing that anymore.'" His mother was upset about it at the time, and in retrospect he still feels guilty about it because they find it very hard now to express emotion to each other. It is just too intimate and embarrassing for them.

Expressing love for our mother is often more difficult for boys, in that kissing our mother first of all violates the "don't be a sissy" subculture of male adolescents, surging with testosterone and trying to gain credibility as "tough guys" by eschewing the soft entanglements of emotion. Often it takes men years of psychotherapy to recover from this ludicrously limited role model of manhood and achieve some connection with this aspect of their emotional lives. Also, of course, our unconscious wars against anything that might hint at incest. Some men are terrified of a moment of tenderness with their mothers, fearing that it could unleash a torrent of longing in them from which they could never escape.

As Mike's mother grows older, he is aware of the growing urgency for resolving this obstacle to their relationship. "When I am alone with my thoughts, I say, 'How long am I going to wait to really show her, or make her feel what I feel for her, before it is too late?' I say that all the time." One day, of course, it *will* be too late. "The moment may never come, and I will be sitting around after she is gone and berating myself about it."

Lerner and Loewe were a world-famous lyric/songwriting partnership for twenty years, and achieved worldwide fame through their music. Loewe became very ill and was dying in the hospital. Lerner went to visit him and realized that in all the years they had written together, he had never told his partner he loved him. He just could not do it. So he went to the oxygen tent, lifted the side, held his partner's hand, and sang the song they had written together:

> I've told every little star,
> just how wonderful you are,
> why haven't I told you?

When I read this story, in a musical review, I thought what a powerful description it was of how difficult it is to say, "I love you"; and of how it is possible to find a way.

A Mother Can Change

Talking about mothers who are "unsung sacrifices" types or mothers who become "martyrs" is not to imply that they are necessarily one way or the other all their lives. People change; lives change. And when that happens with our mother, as when, for example, she becomes a single woman again through divorce or being widowed, it can be an important opportunity to improve our relationship with her. The changes forced on her by fate may facilitate other surprising changes, too.

For Michael Palin, his mother's later life was a revelation. In her teenage and young adult years, her family, who were comfortably off, had groomed her for a sophisticated lifestyle. But when she married, she entered a different world and had to endure quite a difficult marriage. "My parents would row quite a lot. I remember confrontations all the time. Shouting. I thought she was quite hard done by. I remember saying to her once, 'Why don't you divorce?'"

But when Michael's father died, things changed for his mother. "Many people saw his death as a release for her. Dealing with her guilt about being so relieved was probably the worst aspect, but then, after an initial difficult time getting adjusted to being a single woman, she had a very lively last twenty years."

As she got older there were increasing signs of her being able to let her hair down. She enjoyed a life that she had never been able to pursue before. "Nothing illustrates that better than the fact that for her eightieth birthday I took her to New York by Concorde. We got to New York in three hours and eight minutes and I said, 'What do you think?' She said, 'Where do we go now?' I said, 'No, what did you think of the plane?' expecting her to be impressed with the flight. 'Oh, very nice, yes, very nice,' she said. 'Bit noisy.' She'd hardly ever been on a plane, you see, so she thought all planes were like this!"

Michael's mother appeared on television in New York with her famous son. "She didn't know New York at all. It was all new to her, but she absolutely absorbed it. She was able to cope with having a limousine, a driver, and, to cap it all, I think probably the finest moment of her life, she went on *Saturday Night Live* and cohosted the show with me. As you know, the show is a hotbed of spontaneous stuff: it's live and goes out all over America. There are bands playing, and there's my little mother in the middle of it, a tiny, frail figure, reading off cue cards, announcing some wild, druggy band. She went to the party afterward, and at four in the morning she was about the last to go home."

Michael was amazed by the spirit, stamina, and sheer exuberance his mother showed. "Either there was an awful lot of energy which was not used up during a fairly conventional life, which suddenly blossomed at the end, or there is something about old age which just makes you feel less responsible about how you have to behave. That was part of it: most of her life she was behaving well, behaving decently, doing the best thing, being a nurse in the war, working for the Mothers' Union—all that sort of thing. Duty and service were very important to her, not least from the religious angle. As she was an active member of the church, the sanctity of marriage was very, very important. I think it was just great for her to be able to let go and enjoy herself in her last twenty years."

This is an inspiring story about being liberated from the restrictions of unsung sacrifices. Perhaps there are ways each of us can help "liberate" our mother by encouraging her to have adventures large or small that might fill that dream space that for so long she has had to deny.

5 GREAT EXPECTATIONS

The desire to please our mother and make her proud of us is strong in all mother relationships, except those that have irretrievably broken down. If we have a loving relationship with our mother, we want her to be pleased with our achievements because we know that makes her feel happy, at least because it confirms to her that she has been a good mother. If we have a poor relationship with our mother and suspect she does not really love us, we want her to approve of our achievements because it may help her to think us worthy of her love after all.

The Pressure to Achieve

However, many of us feel that, no matter how hard we try, we can never quite match up to our mother's expectations—which are frequently those of both parents.

Mike Pierce's parents were not wealthy, but they worked hard and managed to buy their own home. Mike and his siblings have not matched up to this achievement. "Unfortunately, none of the four of us have been able to do what they've been able to do, as none of us owns a home," Mike said. "My, how times have changed!"

But Mike's suggesting that finding good employment and buying a house is more difficult now than it was in the early 1960s does not find a sympathetic ear with his parents. "They throw our past failures back at us, and say, 'We did it—why can't you?' They have very high expectations about our personal lives as well, which none of us have met: all of us have failed marriages. My mother is very disappointed in us."

Mike resents his parents' attitude toward their grandchildren. "Because they had to burn the candle at both ends to achieve what they did, they really didn't get close to any of us. My oldest sister was the first to have children, but my parents felt she was not involved with the right man, so when she had children they were judged not to be right either; my sister wasn't perfect, and her children weren't perfect. That's what we call our parents—Mr. and Mrs. Perfect."

However, when Mike got married, his parents formed an especially close relationship with his first child. "Once we had our child, we couldn't afford to rent an apartment. This meant we didn't measure up to their standards, but they let us come back to their house to live with them, and my son spent his first years there. They really played with him a lot, and took care of him." After a time Mike felt uncomfortable with this, because it seemed so overdone.

"Because they'd had so little to do with us when we were kids, they overcompensated by throwing all their attention on my son. They still do, because as far as they are concerned, he is the second coming of me! My wife and I are kind of bitter about it, because we've had two more children, whom my parents ignore. We live in our own rented home now, and these two children don't understand why their grandparents never telephone or visit them." It sounds as though Mike's parents think of their grandson as a replacement for Mike, and believe that if they give him plenty of attention, he may be more successful than their son has been—which would reflect on them better. This, of course, also serves to remind Mike of their continuing disappointment in him.

As a psychotherapist, I have observed that such chronic disapproval by parents, which is very common, rarely results in any positive change in an adult child's way of living; rather it induces resentment. If our mother continually harps on about our personal and professional disappointments, as Mike's mother does, nagging references to past "failures" may undermine our future prospects, too. In addition, our mother may need to realize that we fell short of our potential because we were trying too hard to be what she expected of us: We might have done better if we had felt freer to be ourselves.

So if we feel burdened by our mother's expectations, we need to think about them and to decide clearly which we are prepared to meet.

One problem is that if we feel dominated by our mother, we will think of her as "controlling" and "strong," continually placing herself above us. But if we try to understand her point of view, an interesting new perspective may emerge which can help us to alter and improve the way we relate to our mother.

If we have an impasse with our mother, we need to think through what has happened to produce it. Then, when we understand better, we can confront her as an equal and discuss the issues, explaining to her that her expectations seem to be about someone other than us, and that this makes life difficult for us, because if she carries a vision of the child she "expects," she cannot see us for what we are, a person who needs to be understood on our own terms.

As we discuss her expectations, we may learn more about why she has them. Perhaps our mother's own mother had unreasonably hard expectations of her, and so she may be repeating a pattern set for her. Understanding our mother's personal weaknesses and the pressures she has been under herself places her more in perspective. This makes it easier for us to confront her, for we can now think of her as a person like us, rather than as controlling us, a source of guilt-inducing authority.

Also, our mother's point of view may not be what we expect, as looking closely at how other people describe their mother's expectations shows.

The Price of Success

"I remember Mom coming to primary school once and having a meeting with the headmistress," Terry Jones said. "They tried to be secretive about it, but I overheard the headmistress saying, 'You have a gifted child here.'"

We might expect Terry's parents to have been proud of their son. In fact, it was with some apprehension that they accepted his new status. "They were worried. Me writing poetry and everything. They'd all watch TV, but I'd go upstairs and write. Later on I gave them my poetry to read, and they were concerned because it was so gloomy! I was self-motivated, I worked hard, I was terribly serious, and I think they were slightly nervous about me."

Terry's account suggests that the expectations of our parents are not simply about whether or not we reach certain standards and are thereby judged successful. If this was the case, a mother having her child identified as being "gifted" would always respond with happy approval. The fact that she can be made uncomfortable not only by our failure but also by our success shows us that there is another dimension at work. It seems likely in such a case that she expects us to achieve at a certain level, because this is the child she knows; it is the image she has of us. Whether or not her estimation is accurate, if you exceed it, as Terry did, she no longer knows you.

If you suffer, as many of us do, from your mother always expecting something else of you in terms of achievement, remember that the problem may be more to do with her feeling comfortable with you than an absolute judgment of your worth as a person. If you are not measuring up to her expectations, it is not because you are an inadequate person; it is because you are not the person your mother expects.

Something similar happened to me. My older sister died while I was very young, and I found myself bearing my parents' expectations for two children combined into one. The burden took me further and further away from being myself. When I decided to stop worrying about fulfilling the fantasy of what my parents wanted, I felt better off personally. It is never too late to make this resolution. Change is always possible. For example, when I was growing up, I was expected to follow a "sensible" career, perhaps as a schoolteacher, so that I could fit it around my assumed future obligations of being a wife and mother. I did not start my career as a psychotherapist until I was thirty-two, when I went back to college.

Terry Jones's story illustrates that it is possible to achieve far *more* than your mother expected and yet fail to receive the approval you might have expected. John Cleese's experience is similar. His mother says that *Clockwise* is her favorite of all her son's films. When asked why, she said she liked John's role in the film as the headmaster of a school. Her reason for that is revealing.

"I really wanted him to come home and be the headmaster at St. Peter's," she admitted. Despite John's success in both the arts and business, her expectation and hope was that he would return to Weston-super-Mare and take up a teaching post in a local boarding school. In other words, his chosen career is not the one that she expected and would have preferred.

When it became clear that John was not planning to make a career change in order to teach at St. Peter's school, he was amused to receive a letter from his parents asking him if he had ever considered working in Marks & Spencer's personnel department.

So our mother's expectations are not necessarily about achievement in terms of power, fame, and money. They can be tied sometimes to a more intimate and personal model of the child she recognizes and feels comfortable with.

Carla Powell realized early on that she would have to accept the gulf between her mother's expectations and her own dreams. "I saw myself very differently from how my mother saw me," she said. "I always wanted to be independent and always wanted to be *somebody*. I was very much like my grandmother, in fact; I wanted to be an achiever."

Carla's young mind was full of dreams and plans. "I remember as a child I wanted to be married, then I wanted to be a nun, and at nine I wanted to be an actress. She always killed these ambitions instead of encouraging me." I was very good at painting, and I wanted to go to Milan to art college. My mother didn't let me go because she said it was a school for loose girls. I had to go to convent schools instead; I was unhappy at them and I got thrown out of two."

But as Carla grew up, she was able to decide that she did not wish to fulfill expectations that felt alien to her. Today she has on the walls of her house some of her own excellent artwork.

"Funnily enough, it wasn't that difficult," she said. "I

always knew that whatever I was doing, I was never going to satisfy my mother."

We need to realize that if our mother disapproves of us because we have exceeded her expectations, it is unlikely that she will change her view. The answer to this problem is more likely to be found by looking, perhaps with her, at aspects of us that she does approve of. We can ask her to appreciate our good aspects, our best points, and to give us space and time to find our own way. What is it about us that she recognizes as the child she thought she knew? We can suggest that she may be repeating a pattern set by her own mother, and that it is now time for her to break out of it.

What Your Mother Really Wants for You

Colin Powell's visible success in becoming the highest-ranking member of the U.S. Army would seem likely to have met all his mother's expectations. The truth is a little different.

"My mother told all of us, 'Get yourself an education and a job, so that you are supporting yourself,'" Colin said. This was a modest enough expectation—which at first Colin seemed unlikely to fulfill. "Throughout my youth I gave my parents every reason to believe that I might not make it, because I was a very average student. Then I graduated from college, just barely, and went into the army, so that was one expectation met. My mother didn't like the job particularly because she didn't like me being away from New York, and she didn't understand why I would go in the army. 'No one goes into the army!' she said."

For a long time, his army career did not encourage in his mother any higher expectations for him. In fact, compared to other members of his family, he was not doing so well: "I had a number of cousins who excelled far beyond me during the early years, cousins who became lawyers and judges and engineers."

Colin explains that his mother, and others of her generation in his extended family, did not have expectations for their children of prominent career achievement. They expected their children to fulfill more basic achievements of employment, hard work, productivity, raising a family, and decent living, which were more important than individual career "high-flying." This explains why she took his success in her stride. It took quite a while before Colin's army career registered with his mother as an achievement worthy of any particular note: "When I made brigadier general in 1979, I think she realized I had achieved the same level of success as the other more successful cousins, and she then took great pride in her son."

But her measure of his success was on a different scale. "I look at my aunts and uncles, their children and their children's children, and I see three generations of constructive, productive, self-reliant members of society; and all my relatives, whatever their professional status, enjoy equal standing in the family. No cousin stands above another in respect or affection. Some have experienced disappointment, some did not achieve the success they desired, but they all have been successful in what counts in the end. They are all useful human beings: useful to themselves, to their families, to their communities. In other words, in my family system, you didn't have to become chairman of the company, you just had to be a useful contributor to society and not an embarrassment to the family." So Colin's mother is satisfied, and proud, but not the slightest bit overawed by his success.

Nicole Farhi, the successful fashion designer, also thinks her mother is proud of her, but not because she is famous or successful in her job.

"I think she's proud of the way I handle the family: her, my brother, my family, her sisters, my cousins, my daughter. She loves the fact that everything always moves when I'm around. Her brother had an argument years ago with my aunt and her daughters, and then on his birthday I made sure that I invited everybody, the whole family. I put them in the same room and they realized it was stupid to be enemies after so many years. Since then they've all gotten along. I know she liked that."

We need to think carefully about what our mother really expects of us. We may be surprised, and relieved, that her hopes are more humane and less pressuring than we realize.

We also need to remember that sometimes our mother's achievement expectations of us had a positive effect and stemmed from her desire to support us in accomplishing what we set out to do. Jim Clubb's father wanted him to complete his schooling and then join the successful family business. But Jim had always been very interested in animals. "When I was a child, I was crazy about animals and crazy about the circus. I kept a big collection of exotic animals in the garden—snakes, monkeys, fox cubs, things like that—and also when I was thirteen I did a fire-eating act in nightclubs. I did a magic act as well; then I did a cowboy act, whip cracking, knife-throwing, sharpshooting, things like that." When he was seventeen, Jim went on a summer work experience at Chipperfield's circus. "They liked me, and I liked them, and I loved it! I rang home and said, 'I want to leave school and join the circus,' and my mother said, 'Yes, well if that's what he wants to do, let's do it.'"

A mother's support can sometimes come with some cost to her nerves. "Within six months I had become Britain's youngest wild animal trainer. She had a real hard time with it; she was terrified when I started working with lions. She couldn't watch me at first, and when she did finally come to see a show, I remember my father saying beforehand, 'Take it easy with the lions—your mother's watching.' But with all the people out there, they wanted to see a good show, so I had to let them look dangerous!"

Learning to Behave

What we have seen, then, is that our normal understanding of our mother's expectations may be somewhat misguided. They may be more to do with our personal qualities and how we conduct ourselves in relation to others than with worldly success. However, it may perhaps also be useful to direct our attention to our personal qualities, for it may be that we are experiencing some problems with our mother there too. Our mother's expectations concerning aspects of our emotional behavior—for example, how we deal with our anger—can cause difficulties for us as adults.

When we are growing up, our mother teaches us how to fit in with the rest of society, encouraging some kinds of behavior and discouraging and disapproving of others. We are expected to behave in certain ways at the dinner table, in sharing our toys, in crossing the street safely, and in all the other details of our social life. All the little daily approvals and disapprovals that this social training involves burrow deep into our psyche and have a profound effect on the kind of person we become and the way we lead our lives. And of course our mother adds some of her own personal quirks to the societal values she is conditioning us to learn. While this everyday training is benign much of the time, it can become emotionally crippling, especially since much of the training is aimed at moderating the natural exuberance of childhood. To some of us, it can feel as if our mother is trying to place a straitjacket around our emotional self-expression. For example, our childish temper tantrums are a challenge almost every mother has to deal with, by trying to contain extreme outbursts of temper and by setting some firm boundaries. But there is a risk that an overstrict expectation of self-control can lead to the emotional forces underlying our anger.

Janet Peck's mother did not permit her to show anger. "She admonished me all the time to control myself," she said. "'You mustn't raise your voice. Don't shout, don't argue, don't. . .' So the message was that life should be absolute smoothness, and you should keep peace and harmony at any price."

Anger can be a healthy emotion, which we need, for example, in order to assert ourselves when other people are trying to take unfair advantage of us. Obviously, we have to find ways of expressing it which do not physically hurt people or cause unnecessary emotional damage to them; learning how to do this is part of growing up.

However, if our mother always expected us to bottle up our anger, we may be left with a fear of expressing anger even now, as adults. Adults who do not allow themselves to express their anger often become depressed. In addition to being uncomfortable and difficult to bear, depression separates us from other people just as much as the expression of anger which our mother feared. Another danger is that bottled-up anger often escapes in unhealthy ways, either in the form of chronic irritability and blaming, or in unpredictable explosions of rage.

In order to think through an issue like the expression of anger, as usual we should start by trying to see it from our mother's point of view. Anger can be an upsetting emotion, and it is understandable that she feared it. Our childhood outbursts in her presence may have triggered recollections of experiences of her own, and perhaps these carried disturbing echoes of her own parents' anger with her when she was small. These deeper responses might lie below the "peace at any price" strictures of Janet Peck's mother.

Thus our mother might have equated anger with being out of control with rage and therefore been anxious to curb this behavior in us because she did not realize that children learn to handle anger by being allowed to become familiar with the emotion within the context of firm boundaries.

There may be more prosaic reasons for her placing limits on us. For little girls especially, many mothers fear that displays of temper will make them unattractive and ugly. Even in these times, when gender roles are becoming less entrenched, girls still seem to be more constrained in acting out, while boys may be encouraged to be freer with their anger since it is consistent with the stereotypical expectation that they should grow up to be assertive, effective men. Sometimes, if our childhood anger was directed at our mother, her disapproval may have simply been self-defensive; she felt that she did not deserve it after all she did for us, and that we had no right to make her a target of anger.

As adults, we may feel that the negative effects of being forced to bottle up our anger are much worse for us than the outcomes our mother feared. It is certainly true that repressed anger usually carries with it a host of associated emotional entanglements, mostly unpleasant. For instance, if we feel that our mother overcontrolled our expression of anger, our resentment about this might take the form of anger directed toward her, and many of us feel guilty about being angry with our mother.

The restrictive way in which Janet Peck's mother raised her also found its way into other areas of her self-expression. While many mothers put pressure on their children, especially girls, to look well turned out, in Janet's case her mother's expectations went in the other direction. Pride in appearance was seen as vanity: "I was never praised for being pretty or concerned about how I looked," she said. "The reaction would be, 'Well, no one's going to be looking at you!' so I didn't have any confidence that anyone would be looking at me, and so therefore I didn't develop any later on, when social confidence became important."

For Janet, not being vain translated into not expecting to have nice clothes. "Her excuse for buying me secondhand clothes was financial hardship: 'This might not be what you want but this is what I can afford.'" Janet felt that her mother's attitude went beyond the realistic bounds of living within a tight budget and became more an approach to life in general— a defeatist, joyless way of being. "It was this way all the time, and so my confirmation dress had to be homemade, out of cheaper material, and it did not look as white as the other girls' dresses. My mother said, 'This is the best we can do.' You could feel her sense of martyrdom: 'Life is so hard we can't have the nice things, and don't you forget it.' It was never expressed verbally like that, but that was the message."

When Janet passed an exam to get into grammar school, her success was dramatically symbolized by her new school uniform. "Up to then my clothes always came from jumble sales and things. The only new outfit I ever had was my school uniform, which the social services bought for me when I passed the exam. It was one of the absolute turning points in my life."

Janet's account of her childhood relationship with her mother demonstrates how her sense of confidence and self-worth were chronically undermined. As we grow up, we internalize the ways our mother relates to life and repeat them in our own lives. We need to become aware of how such patterns were created before we can try to change them. One reason it takes time to develop this awareness is that extreme containment of self-expression can be disguised as something more reasonable, such as Janet's mother's frugality. If we feel our mother's expectations have caused us to repress emotions, whether anger or other strong feelings, in thinking through our psychological history, it is important to allow ourselves the time and space to *feel* these emotions, without fear and without guilt. To feel strong emotions is not wrong. If we become used to feeling them and get to know them, there is less danger that they will affect our behavior unconsciously, leading us to do and say things that we then regret.

As we become more aware of what we have been conditioned to repress, it is natural we feel sad, angry, and resentful; but blaming our mother does nothing to improve matters. It is more useful to us to understand the states of mind that caused our mother's behavior. If we can realize some of the possible explanations for our mother's behavior it is more likely that, even if her actions were mistaken, we will be able to see them as understandably mistaken. "I think it was all about her own lack of self-confidence," Janet said of her mother's constraint. "She hadn't got any to impart to me." It helps to put our mother's motives for the expectations she set in the best possible light—to consider, for instance, that perhaps she was no good at these aspects of mothering because of her own weaknesses, insecurities, and worries. She may have tried to mother us, even though she ended up damaging us. If we can, it is much healthier for us to give our mother the benefit of the doubt, to believe that she did her best for us even though it was not very good, and to forgive her. Our energy is better spent on working to improve those aspects of our emotional world that were left lacking by her shortcomings than by wasting it on blaming her.

I'm Not a Child Anymore

Like many of us, Ann Watson was a better-behaved adolescent at home than she was when out with her friends, trying to conform to her mother's expectations when with her while being her naturally more rebellious teenage self elsewhere. "I think I put on faces when I was an adolescent," she told me. "I was a very good actor. I wanted my parents to think one thing about me, and yet to live another kind of life. I wanted to be the good girl at home and the bad girl outside, and I managed pretty well."

Until her two worlds suddenly intersected, that is. "I was never like 'evil bad,'" she explained. "It was more like trying things on. But I remember when my mother caught me smoking a cigarette outside my high school. I was taking a break from rehearsing a school play, when she happened to walk by. She saw me, but didn't speak to me. I panicked. I didn't know what to do. I tossed the cigarette under a car and thought, 'She didn't see me,' but I knew she had." Silent disapproval was the method Ann's mother used to get her daughter to conform to her expectations.

Eventually Ann became more rebellious at home, too. "I remember when she caught my sister and me getting high, smoking a joint in my bedroom. She didn't speak to us for two days. I think she didn't know what to say, so she didn't say anything. So we got the silent treatment. She was angry. It was never that she stopped loving me; it was more a case of 'You're not doing it right.'"

As Ann became an older teenager and expressed herself more fully, the silent treatment mode of showing disapproval gave way to more open arguments. "I was pretty wild with the way I dressed by the time I was at high school," she told me. "I went through a punk rock phase and my mother couldn't stand it. I would wear these sheer dresses and no slip underneath, and she would be on me like, 'People can see your legs!' and I would say, 'Well, what do they *think* are under the dress?'"

Ann says the disputes were more to do with her mother

reacting to expectations of how her teenage daughter should look than with important matters of principle. "It was all to do with appearances; they were very important to my mother—how things looked on the outside. Didn't matter if you were falling apart on the inside, as long as everything was all right on the outside."

These sorts of disputes with our mother must be almost universal today. Our mother has absorbed expectations, from within her own generation, of what is acceptable behavior and what is not. Frequently as adolescents we perceive these rules and regulations as trivial and superficial, and not reflective of our individual wishes and the fashions of our subculture. And while most mothers try to understand and adapt to the mores of their children's generation, the gap between mother and children, particularly during the teenage years, is so common as to seem almost built in to such relationships in the modern era.

The progression of teenage behavior is usually as Ann has described it: being a good son or daughter at home, but with freer expression outside; then being caught by mother in a compromising situation outside home, thus dispelling the illusion of childlike goodness; then behaving more daringly at home; and finally as an adolescent asserting the right to self-expression in such matters as dress, hairstyle, and so on. Despite, or perhaps because of, the disputes, the result is a movement toward adult individuality.

The problem for many of us, however, is that our mother never quite accepts this healthy progression. Our relationship with her can still be spoiled by continual wrangles over her disapproval of the way we are living our life. It is as if the "You're not doing it right" admonition from our earlier years still haunts us. This niggling (often over minor matters such as our dress, our choice of curtains, or whether we smoke or not) can induce a surprisingly strong level of resentment, because it echoes our dependency on her during our childhood and adolescent years, reminding us that she does not respect our maturity as adults.

If this is our situation, we must discuss it with our mother. We need first to remind her of the fact that we are no longer a child, and expect to be treated as an adult. Next, we need to reassure our mother that we value her opinion but would like her to reserve her views until we ask for them.

As we have seen, our mother's expectations, in which she wants us to be better or different from the way we are, can be the source of much torment. In trying to deal with this by thinking through why she behaves toward us as she does, we may understand some of her weaknesses. It is never easy to forgive, for we are aware of the hurt we have suffered, but understanding some of her weaknesses makes it easier to forgive her.

In considering forgiveness, we should remember that at the root of the problem of her expectations is the fact that our mother could not accept us as we are, with our imperfections. To forgive her, we have to accept her as she is, with *her* imperfections. If we cannot, we are repeating her pattern. If we can, we are breaking the pattern and moving to a healthier relationship with our mother.

6 RED-HOT MAMAS

At about the age of ten, I began singing in the church choir. The sermons seemed long and boring, so during them I used to peruse the congregation. I would see Mr. Redeker asleep again, or even, on one embarrassing occasion, my father too. One day, gazing at the pews full of people in their Sunday-best clothes, I spotted an attractive woman in a pale blue cloche hat. After a few seconds, I realized that it was my mother. I saw for the first time that she was very pretty, and that she was rather more well endowed than some of the other ladies. Becoming aware of her as an attractive woman was a kind of awakening for me, for as a child I had not been conscious of her sexuality.

At this time my mother started explaining to me about love and sex, but I had already learned a lot at school that seemed much more interesting: my school friends were talking about people being naked with each other in bed! My sermon observations began to veer toward fantasy; I would imagine Mrs. Tilley or Mr. Hidlebald in bed without their clothes on, rubbing up and down, and doing things I had not quite, as yet, fully understood.

Most of us have memories of the arrival of the world of sexuality into our lives. It marked a particularly important stage in our relationship with our mother; our preoccupation with sexual matters, coupled with our increasing independence, formed a potent cocktail that most mothers found difficult to handle. Moreover, conflicts that arose with our mother over sexual matters often symbolized wider differences between us. Understanding—through issues raised by the interviews for this book—some of what happened as we grew up sexually can help us to understand our relationship with our mother better, and perhaps to see more clearly the basis of problems that we may be having with her today.

Growing Up Is Growing Away

Ryan O'Connell's mother was a strict supervisor of his social life. "It made my adolescence difficult, in the sense that I had to lie to her for years about where I was going and what I was doing. Looking back, I realize that she meant well, and now I feel bad about all the lies. But I had to do it."

Being economical with the truth about our social and sexual life was the norm for many of us. Most of our mothers found the role of sounding board for our adolescent confidences one they could not or would not fulfill; or, even if they were willing, we were not. But some of us were able to find another mother figure with whom we could share intimate information. She might have been another family member, an older sister, or an aunt—or someone outside our family.

For Ryan this figure was his best friend's mother. "Gretchen lived around the block from me. She was the coolest lady. For a fifty-year-old lady she was something else! She wasn't strict with her three sons, my friends—they could do whatever they wanted. And I could go and tell Gretchen anything—anything! Women, sex, drinking . . . what I told her went way beyond what I would tell my mother."

For most of us, entering the world of adolescent sexuality was commonly associated with a feeling that we were growing away from our mother into a world she could not share. Natural though this is, some of us had mothers who could not accept our increasing need for privacy.

"I remember the biggest crisis in our house was when I was seventeen or eighteen years old," said Wes Crow. "My mother was a cleaning freak, always putting things away and straightening things up. One day she came across a letter that had some reference to smoking pot. She flipped out, searched all over my room, and found an empty pack of condoms. She became hysterical. She was so upset she wouldn't speak to me. As a consequence, my dad took me out for a walk. He started talking to me about drugs, and then said, 'But son, what your mom's really upset about is the pack of condoms.' I thought, 'Well, I'm a guy, and at least I'm *using* these things!' Since then I've never brought up the subject of sex with my mother, and I always felt she was harshly judging any girl I was dating, assuming I was sleeping with her."

The episode features in Wes's memory as a "bit of a trauma, though not a serious one." It left a sense of injustice, both because his privacy had been invaded by his mother searching his room and because he felt that he had been behaving perfectly normally for a young man of his age. An invasion of privacy can also cause mistrust between a mother and an adolescent child, which makes it difficult for the adolescent to ask their mother for advice about important sexual matters such as pregnancy, venereal disease, or AIDS.

Our mother's attitude to sex at this stage of our lives has an intense effect on us because it is contained within a closed system; it is not until we become old enough to have a peer subculture, in which we are able to discuss these issues more openly with our friends, that the influence of our mother lessens.

Sexual behavior also serves as an arena for heightening differences between us and our mother in other areas of our growing up. For example, even in a liberal home environment, sexual matters could create problems because our mother found it difficult to change her perception of us as we moved from being a child to an adolescent, with all the accompanying personality changes; we may have a sense—which can last well beyond adolescence—that our mother has not accepted that we are growing up. We, on the other hand, had become used to seeing our mother as an authority figure, a guiding presence, and knowing we were straying into territory beyond her jurisdiction might have plunged our relationship with her into confusion. Sometimes the ensuing conflicts erected barriers between us and our own mothers that continue to affect our relationship today.

So conflict over sexual matters might often have become complicated by issues of our mother's power and control over us. When we became adolescents, our focus switched to our peer subculture. While our parents could still be important, they were now only one influence among many. This was difficult for our mother, because she sensed a lessening of her control over us just as we started to change rapidly. Wes's story illustrates possible areas of conflict between our young adult self and our mother, some of which last into adulthood, and each of which can have consequences for how we get along with her today: our needs for privacy, to be respected as adults, to be accepted as sexual beings, and to to be allowed to conduct our personal relationships without interference.

Our Mother and Our Privacy

When he was a teenager, Brendan Glover's mother carried out a similar "search and find" raid on his bedroom. He was very much in love with his girlfriend, and used to compose poems to her, laboring hard on them to achieve perfect meter and rhyme. He kept the rough drafts of his poems in a notebook, which he hid by stuffing it under his mattress. "One day," he said, "I took out my notebook to work on some poems, and I realized that my mother had discovered it, because the poems had been edited—Mom had corrected the grammatical errors! I can just imagine her standing there next to my bed," he added wryly, "unable to resist meddling, but trying to justify it to herself: 'It's for his own good.'"

Mothers are often tempted to invade their adolescent children's privacy in order to gain access to their teenager's secret life: to find out what they are up to and to try to maintain control over a world that used to be open to them but has become increasingly hidden. The resentment it causes can still underlie tensions between us and our mother today. If you felt the invasion of your teenage privacy keenly, and it still affects your relationship with your mother, it may help to think through your memory of the events and the circumstances surrounding them. In trying to understand such behavior better, it helps us to bear in mind that there are several major anxieties facing mothers of teenagers. A mother might fear that, as her child grows up and becomes a sexually functioning person, she will lose control of her child's behavior. Also, because our sexual activity signals that we are maturing into a more adult phase of our life, she can feel herself being moved on in the life cycle; it also signals her own aging and she may not welcome the sense of her own mortality that comes with recognizing that fact.

We should also remember that it is easy for mothers to come across personal information by accident. Once when I was changing the sheets on my teenage son's bed, I found porn magazines hidden under the mattress. "Ooops," I thought, "what am I going to do? I can't tell him I didn't change the sheets!" I didn't want to take the magazines away from him because they seemed to be harmless, so I put them back as carefully as I could. Of course, I probably put them back incorrectly, and so he very likely realized I had seen them, and thought, "She's being snoopy." Some of our mother's invasions of our privacy were probably of this kind. Of course, repeated invasions of our privacy is another matter, and maybe not all her invasions were fortuitous; nevertheless, if, like many adolescents, we were extremely sensitive to this issue, we may remember her as more purposely invasive than she really was.

This story also illustrates that while our mother might invade our privacy, she may also turn a blind eye to sexual matters; indeed, she may have done so more often than we realized. And our mother's ignoring a sexual matter of which she might be expected to disapprove can happen right into adulthood, as Alexander Scott-Irvine's experience shows. He had lived openly as a homosexual since leaving home, and his mother had met his partner many times when the two of them visited her. Nevertheless, she did not seem to acknowledge the significance of their relationship and continued to ask Alexander whether he had a girlfriend and when he might marry and have children. Alexander was noncommittal and did not attempt to explain things to his mother.

One summer Alexander decided to invite his mother to visit him and his partner in London. It was not until she was about to arrive that Alexander realized the possible consequences of her visiting the one-bedroom apartment they shared, which had only a double bed. What should he do? Tell her he was gay? He finally decided to not say anything. "Well, she arrived," Alexander said. "She looked around the apartment, went into the bedroom, said what a lovely place it was, and then we went out to dinner!"

When a mother turns a blind eye in this way, she is tacitly acknowledging that her adult child has an independent life, and it is not necessarily appropriate for her views, critical or otherwise, to be voiced.

Sometimes our mother's turning a blind eye can be a little more obvious. Nick Briggs remembers his nineteenth birthday party, which was also a going away party as he was shortly leaving for college. "I was very drunk, and had gone up to my bedroom with a girlfriend, closed the door, and turned out the light. It was getting late, and downstairs my godmother was ready to leave the party and go home. She wanted to say goodbye to me, so my mother came up to find me and walked into my bedroom. I was sitting on my bed with my girlfriend giving me a blow-job. She turned on the light and went 'Oh!' turned off the light, shut the door, and stood outside. 'Er, Nicholas, your godmother's leaving ... could you please hurry and come?' Classic. She had no idea what she'd said, of course. And she's never mentioned the incident since."

When Our Mother Respects Us as Adults

Most of us expect our mother to be conservative in matters surrounding the body and sexuality. Certainly Marilyn Cole did; her mother was quite old-fashioned. Marilyn lived with her parents and two sisters in a small house, but, she said,

"Amazingly enough we did not see each other naked. We were all very modest about our bodies."

Marilyn thought this might be a problem when she got a modeling assignment. "I left home, and I'd only been in London two weeks when I was invited to model for *Playboy* in Chicago. I thought I'd better tell my parents. I said to my mother, 'I'm going to pose for this magazine called *Playboy*, Mom.' She said, 'It's one of *those* magazines, isn't it?' expressing concern and disapproval. I replied, 'Yes, it is. But don't worry, they drape you in things.' So she said, 'Er, okay.' But then the magazine decided to make me the centerfold, totally naked. They gave me a little Polaroid picture from the shoot to take back with me, and when I went home I thought, 'I'll have to show them the photo.' When I showed it to them, Mom totally ignored the fact that I was stark naked, and said, 'Ooh, doesn't your hair look nice!' We never discussed it any further. That's how we got over it."

Her parents came not only to accept it, but even to be proud. "*Playboy* stuff, at that time, was big news. And they were photographed in the *Daily Telegraph* supplement. There they were, my mom and dad on their little sofa, looking at my centerfold, holding it up. The press wanted a story of a disapproving mum, but they didn't get it!"

This story is of a mother who has accepted her daughter as an adult in her own right. Clearly she did not really approve of Marilyn being photographed for *Playboy*, but she did not try to impose her views—and she went further than turning a blind eye in that she publicly acknowledged what her daughter was doing. Perhaps when a mother can allow her adult child the freedom to make her own decisions, it also enables her to suspend her previous inhibitions. Marilyn was successful on her own terms, her mother felt able to go with it, and wholeheartedly enjoy her daughter's success.

Such acceptance would probably not have extended as far as Marilyn's grandmother, though. "Mom's mom, at the time, was in her eighties, and she used to go to church twice on a Sunday. Between services she would come and have Sunday lunch at Mom's house. I happened to be at home one weekend, and when she saw me she said, 'Mrs. So-and-so at t'church told me you're doin' trapeze work in London.' We stared at Gran and we thought, 'What's she talking about?' Then we realized: someone had said 'striptease'! I said, 'Gran, I swear to you, I am not doing trapeze work in London.' And we left it at that."

Relating to Our Newfound Sexuality

Marilyn's mother was able to accept her as adult, but not all mothers are able to deal well with their daughters becoming sexual beings.

For Emma Parsons, this happened because her mother did not make any allowance for the fact that she was different from her brothers. While sometimes it is assumed that there are significant gender differences between the attitudes that mothers take toward the sex lives of their sons and daughters, in the interviews for this book there were surprisingly few examples of clear-cut differences. "I used to get upset when people said, 'It must be wonderful to be the only girl in the family, with three brothers.' I was treated the same way as everybody else; there wasn't any special place in my parent's affections because I was a girl. I didn't get any sense of being different."

This attitude became a problem when she was dealing with significant events in her feminine development. "The feminine things were not acknowledged, so the business of my periods starting was awful. I hadn't been warned about it, so of course I thought I was dying, or had some terrible thing wrong with my insides. I was scared."

Because of her mother's inability to relate to her sensitively at this stage of her life, Emma's experience of puberty was difficult. "When my mother told me what it was, the way she told it made the experience seem grubby and horrible. I can remember my depression, and thinking, 'It's so unfair being a girl. If this is going to happen every single month of my life, I can't bear it.' I was furious. I was a tomboy anyway, and I despised girlish things."

Geoff Minter's mother was no more understanding or sensitive with her daughter in sexual matters. He remembered, "Our mother was a little more hands-off with me, because she didn't really understand an adolescent boy. But with my sister, her attitude was that she knew what a girl was, and how her life should be run, so she was much harder on her. When Kerry got her hair cut in a way that my mother didn't like, there was a huge argument, with Mom going through the house and taking down every mirror, yelling at her, 'You're too hideous-looking for even *you* to see!'"

Her mother's overreaction and concern with her daughter's appearance suggest an inability to accept her developing sexuality and physical attractiveness—a difficulty in their relationship that became pronounced when as a late teenager, Geoff's sister lost her virginity. "Kerry was very careful and used a diaphragm. One day, Mom was going through Kerry's drawers—she'd regularly go through our drawers, saying, 'If you're honest, you have nothing to hide'—and she found the diaphragm. She waited for Kerry to get home, then summoned her: 'Kerry!' Kerry claimed that she had the diaphragm in preparation for when she was older, and that nothing had happened. But Mom said, 'Well, then, let's see your tube of diaphragm jelly, unopened.' In tears, Kerry went upstairs to the bathroom, slammed the door and locked it, found the tube of jelly and started trying to squeeze toothpaste into it to fill it back up! I don't think my mother believed her, but a reasonable degree of doubt was established, and she was off the hook."

Interfering with Our Personal Relationships

While Kerry's experience with her mother concerns her mother's attitudes toward her as a sexual being, it is also bound up with other aspects of their relationship: her mother's need to control her. "For my sister, our mother's supervision extended even into adulthood," Geoff said; "what clothes she should buy, how she should wear her hair, how she should put on her makeup. Kerry recently had a baby, and our mother went to be with her for the first two weeks of the baby's life: you know, ostensibly to help. But of course the subliminal purpose was to oversee and make sure everything is being done 'right,' meaning according to her wishes: 'This milk is not warm enough,' 'You're taking another shower? You're obsessed with cleanliness' and so forth."

As a psychotherapist, I have seen that mothers who feel

confident and secure in themselves do not feel the need to control their adult children. But less mature mothers may feel abandoned by their children as they grow up, and so cannot let go of the need to stay in control. In a sense, such a mother cannot grow with her children to reach the next stage of her own life, and so she clings on to the only role she knows and behaves as though she were still a mother of small children.

When he was a young man, Geoff's mother tried to exert an influence on his social life with girls, with some pointed comments about their failings: "Well, she's not the prettiest woman you've ever dated." He finally had to draw some boundaries. "When I was about twenty-six, I had to tell her, 'When I'm ready to marry a woman, I'll let you know; then I'll ask your blessing. But until then. . .' and after that there was no problem."

If our mother tries to influence our lives and relationships, we should take the time to think through all the topics she brings up. We need to assess each one, being careful not to reject her advice out of hand just because it is coming from her, but instead to examine it with care. Once we have decided whether or not to accept her advice, we can either go our own quiet way with it, or confront her and explain that we prefer to do things our own way. We may feel reluctant to reject her advice, in case we hurt her feelings, but in fact, this drawing of boundaries can be helpful for our mother. It is often difficult for her to make smooth adjustments to her understanding of what is appropriate for her to say and do, as we grow more adult; so she may welcome guidance from us on when we want her advice and when we do not.

It is not always possible, though, to change our mother's behavior in relationship to our personal affairs. When Bill

Goldman, whose mother was Jewish, married a woman whose mother was a southern Baptist, there was trouble. "My mother was horrified; Eileen was a Gentile, and suddenly my mother became very Jewish, which she wasn't normally. But Eileen was so beautiful, and so winning, that eventually my mother, who would have been nice to Hitler if he had been nice to her, began to talk to my wife." But it was a harder battle with his wife's mother. "Eileen was Texan. When she met me, she wrote her mother a letter telling her about me, and about my being a writer. Her mother called her up and said, 'He sounds fabulous. The only thing is, you never mentioned his name.' Eileen said, 'It's Bill Goldman.' There was a long pause. 'Is that his pen name?' Anyway, we went to Dallas to meet her and I tried to make conversation. She was not about to speak to anyone who was Jewish. So I would say, 'Gee, what are those, cows?' and my mother-in-law would say, 'Eileen, aren't those heifers?' She would never talk to me or answer my questions directly."

It can be hard if we are on the receiving end of such absurd behavior, but it can help us to remember that it probably has less to do with us as a person than it has to do with our mother's issues of control. In such a situation, provided our partner is prepared to ignore our mother's attempts to impose her views, we should take a relaxed perspective and treat the problem as our mother's. Bill and Eileen did, and eventually Bill and his mother-in-law got along much better.

Understanding Your Mother's Affairs

When Daniel Abraham was a child, his mother had a female friend whose husband was a romantic figure who made a lot of money. "Every time we passed by his apartment building," Daniel recalled, "she used to say, 'Charles Salet lived there.' I always knew there was something special between them. I was only about eight, nine, ten years old and yet I knew that something had happened."

"Something had happened"—a sense, a feeling, a hunch about something to do with our mother. Often it turns out, on adult reflection, to have been instinctively right. Such impressions are incomplete to us as children. Our knowledge about the adult world of our mother was a kaleidoscope of little bits of knowledge, hints and clues, suspicions and information that we did not fully understand—like the fact that our parents had a sex life.

Discovering that they did can be a complex and difficult process. When we first realize that our mother is a sexual person, we may feel intense interest in the subject; we think we want to know everything. But often we also feel fearful that we might discover too much; we do not want to accept that our mother might be involving herself in this activity. Childlike, we often decide to repress what we know about our mother as a sexual being, and preserve her in our mind as a madonna figure.

When we became adults, and realized that our parents have or had a sex life, this discovery can be difficult to cope with. It is surprising how long the image of a mother without sex, separate, pure, and unsullied by a man, can stay with us through life. Alexander Scott-Irvine's father is now dead. When he was asked how he would respond if his mother remarried, he became flustered and said, "She just couldn't do that. I would be very upset." When challenged that his attitude seemed to be contradictory, for he expected her to be open-minded enough to accept that he is gay, but he was not open-minded enough himself to accept her remarriage, he simply said emphatically, "That's different!"

When Richard Eyre was sorting out his mother's belongings shortly after her death, he came across a suitcase full of letters. "They were letters from my father to my mother, written during World War II," he explained. "I guess there were about a thousand of them." Richard couldn't read them at first, because it seemed such an invasion of his mother's privacy. When he eventually did, he was shocked. "They were extraordinarily sexually frank; I mean, these letters were about their sexual relationship." The letters were obviously for his mother's titillation. Richard reckoned that this eroticism had been fueled by the fact that his father was away in the navy during the war, where the risks and dangers made life more intense. "I stopped reading. I thought, 'I am not up to coping with this.'"

Shocked though Richard was by the intensity and nature of the secret, as often happens when we learn about our mother's past, he already "knew something." He had been aware as a teenager of an "extra dimension" to his parents' sex life. "You see, I knew, when I was a teenager, that they were competitively having affairs. And then my father would try and seduce my girlfriends, and my mother would try and seduce my sister's boyfriends."

Charlotte Duncan's mother's sexual affairs affected her severely. She described her relationships with the opposite sex as incredibly difficult because of her mother's transgressions. "My mother was extremely pretty and glamorous. The 1950s were her years. She wore those kinds of frocks, makeup, and curly hair. We never got along well—there was a gulf between her perception of the world and mine. And then one day, as a teenager, I discovered that she was sleeping with one of my boyfriends."

Charlotte got over the shock, and has tried to come to terms with it. "After all, who really is fit to be a mother?" she said. "We all make terrible mistakes. We have to live with them and should not berate ourselves." Charlotte regrets, now that her mother is dead, that they did not have a better relationship. "Given time I think we could have made our peace but she was diagnosed with Alzheimer's in her early fifties, just as I was ready to make the attempt. When she died twenty years later in a nursing home, I stood over her and said, 'I'm sorry, Mother— I never said a nice thing to you in your life.' No mother deserves that."

Given the nature of her mother's involvement with her adolescent sexual life, Charlotte has come to a remarkably clear point of understanding. She can forgive her mother for her transgressions and manages to see life in a larger perspective.

Once again, we need to remember that forgiving our mother does not mean that we are sanctioning what she did or repressing knowledge of what happened. It means simply that we recognize her for the vulnerable and flawed person we all are in one way or another, and that we must then try to move on. Charlotte's example is important for those of us who are struggling with our mothers over the emotional legacy of our adolescent sexuality.

For Monica Benton, her mother's past was also hard to cope with. When she was a young woman, Monica discovered that her mother's relationship with her own father, Monica's grandfather, had been dangerously close to incest; indeed, it might have crossed the line. "She is a paradox!" Monica began. "She's English and upper-class, and yet there are aspects of her that you might not expect from someone of her upbringing. She's an anarchist about sex and relationships with men."

Unusually for those days, Monica's mother did not marry until her midthirties. "She'd had many opportunities to marry and didn't. When she did finally marry, her father, my grandfather, was distraught. Before giving her away, he drove her around the church eighteen times, telling her that she needn't go through with it, and could just forget the whole thing and leave with him. Their relationship was extremely intense, more intense than I care to contemplate."

Although the relationship between Monica's mother and her grandfather was never discussed between Monica and her mother when she was young, her mother told her about it when she grew up. Monica now wishes she had not. "I don't think she has ever perceived the potency of any of this. She's told me more than I wanted to know, in a sense, because my grandfather really brought me up. I didn't go to school, and he educated me for quite a few years. I remember spending years of my life with him, sitting on a chaise-longue between his legs, while he read to me. It felt absolutely innocent, but once I knew this thing about him and my mother, it sort of colored that childhood experience in an unpleasant way. I resented her for telling me. Somehow deep in my soul I didn't quite believe it. But looking back now, I think it probably was like that."

The huge subject of parental, or grandparental, sexual abuse of children is complex and there is not space in this book to deal with it directly; it is only possible to advise in general terms. If you had an experience like this that left you feeling disturbed, it may be helpful to think it through and try to clarify the details so they are not distorted. Then you have to decide, as an adult, whether you would feel better if you explored it, or whether you would prefer to keep it hidden. If you decide you want to explore further, you can, if you wish, seek professional advice. This does not mean that you are emotionally unstable; it does mean that you are taking the sensible precaution of obtaining skilled help in untangling a web of memories that can be disturbing. In addition, in deciding how to deal with upsetting memories and in talking about them with family members, you need to be careful about involving others in the process who would otherwise be innocent of the matter, as Monica was when her mother told her of her relationship with her grandfather. This is of course a matter of personal judgment, for each situation is unique.

In thinking through how as young adults we were affected by our mother, it can sometimes be useful to find out about our own mother's sex and love history, even though this can sometimes be upsetting. Matters of love are so important to us all and can affect us so deeply that they never cease to be a challenge; we can be sure that our mother has struggled herself. It is all too easy for us to think back with resentment to how, for instance, our mother used to restrict our sex life and to forget all the other issues involved that may have complicated matters for her—dealing with sexual taboos from her own upbringing, her adult sexual affairs, seeing our growing maturity as a sign of her own aging, and so on. Understanding more about her experiences may help to loosen up our thinking and give us a clearer perspective on any disruptions to our relationship then that may still be relevant to it today.

7 DARK SECRETS

In the interviews for this book,

many people talked spontaneously about finding

out their mother's secrets and what a dramatic

impact these discoveries had on them. For many,

the existence of the secret itself was a shock. The

fact that there had been information concealed from them as children left them feeling let down, even betrayed, by their mother. This chapter considers some of the things our mothers know, or knew, but did not share with us: her personal matters, information about us, or family secrets.

To improve our relationship with our mother we need to understand the potency of such hidden knowledge, the impact on us of discovering things we were not meant to know, and how as adults we can ask our mother to tell us what she has hidden for so long. If we can see why secrets are generally established, we will better understand how to approach our mothers to reveal hers; and if we understand how the keeping of secrets can damage us, we will know better how to resolve their legacy in our adulthood.

Why Didn't She Tell Me the Truth?

One Christmas Day, when Tony Cox was a young boy, his drunk father crashed his car through their front gate. "It shocked me," Tony said. "I didn't actually see it, I just heard it. I was told to stay in my room."

Tony's mother had always tried to conceal from him his father's heavy drinking. "She usually hid it from me brilliantly," he said. "She would time things to perfection, sending me round somewhere to play when she knew when he was coming home." But increasingly, as incidents like the Christmas Day crash became frequent, Tony's father foiled his mother's attempts to draw a curtain over his drunkenness. The heavy drinking affected all aspects of family life, as Tony's mother tried to organize everything around the need to keep it secret from Tony. The lie expanded as all members of the family pretended not to notice that anything was out of the ordinary.

The drinking got worse. Then Tony's father tried to kill his wife. "When I was about seven, he nearly strangled her. My aunt, who was living with us, woke me, screaming, 'He's trying to kill her!' I never saw him do it, but it was so near me." The violent struggle took place in the room next to Tony's bedroom, but he was shielded from it by his mother, who told him to stay in his room. "It must have been pretty horrific. I can't imagine my father doing that, but then I never really saw him so drunk as to make him want to kill her."

Many mothers keep information from us for our own protection, as Tony's did. But the stress and strain of doing so can begin to tell. Tony feels that the burden of secrets his mother had to keep contributed to her early death from cancer. "She worried all the time. Everything was really private, and she didn't want to show me any personal problems." She always told Tony that everything was going to be all right, no matter how bad things were.

Tony understands that his mother was trying to protect him. However, he believes adamantly that as he grew older he should have been told more. He would rather have shared some of the burden of her secrets: "I wish she'd told me. I would still rather have known." This was important to his need as an adult to have a clear perception of his parents. "People tend to keep seeing parents as parents, and they're not just that. They're people, and they're living a life."

One of the ways in which secrets kept by our mother can damage us is that they can cause us unnecessary guilt. Tony cannot bear to visit his mother's grave. "I know where she's buried. I've never been there. I can't bring myself to do it. I don't want to open that door, because as I get older I realize what problems she had, and I feel bad that she died before I could share them with her."

If, like Tony, we were aware that our mother kept secrets hidden from us that we could have shared, it can help to find out about them now. Even in retrospect finding out connects us with a missing dimension of our life with our mother. It may be difficult for our mother to share her secrets; even now she may not be able to admit them to herself and deal with them directly; or she may have locked some secrets away because she was not able to express her emotions, or perhaps was afraid to communicate her unhappiness. But it may be that our mother would welcome the chance to talk about issues that have been buried for so long and, if we can overcome the difficulties, asking our mother might at the very least prevent some of the sort of guilt and pain Tony felt about not knowing. His mother is now dead, but there is one question he says he would ask her, if he could. "I would ask her why she didn't tell me how it really was," he replied. "The truth."

Don't Tell Anyone Our Business

Bill Goldman knew the truth right from the beginning. His father drank too, but his mother did not conceal it from him; rather, she required him and his brother to keep their father's alcoholism secret from the rest of the world.

Bill described how his father's alcoholism began. His father had enjoyed working as vice president of the Chicago Mail

Order Company for many years, but his mother feared that the company would fire him before retirement age, and so convinced him he should leave and go into business for himself. "He did not want to retire, but he did so because my mother wanted him to, and she was the powerful one in the family." Bill's father formed his own company, but being the head of it was beyond his capabilities and eventually destroyed him. "It turned out that my father was someone who needed to have a company around him; he was not someone who was ever meant to be a leader." He turned to drink. "We got a call from his partner saying that my father was hopelessly drunk in a motel room. Eventually the company self-destructed because of his drinking, and he lived the last six years of his life upstairs at home, drunk."

When his father was drinking, no sound came from his bedroom; there was just an ominous silence. Periodically, he would run out of drink and have to sober up. "We would have family meetings in the dining room and he would say, 'I'm going to be good from now on—no more liquor, I promise you, I swear,' and he would be sober for a day, a week, or a month. Then I would come home from school, and the silence would be back. He would be upstairs, drinking again.

"He used to buy an infinite amount of tiny liquor bottles, half pints and what we would call 'airplane bottles,' and he hid them all over the house. I remember once, when it got really bad, my mother coming in screaming, 'Find the bottles, find the bottles—I'll give you fifty cents for every bottle you find!' My father was staggering around the room saying, 'Don't do it!' so drunk that he was falling against the walls. I didn't know who to please or what to do, so I rooted around in various drawers and closets, and found this bottle and that bottle, but I'm sure I didn't find all of them."

Bill's mother was terrified that if anyone found out about her husband's drinking she would be socially humiliated. "That was the reason for the huge family secret," Bill said.

All families have some innocent secrets from the outside world. Inside jokes and shared traditions and experiences help to cement the identity of a family and to create an informal boundary around it. But in his book *The Secret Life of Families,* family therapist Evan Imber-Black considers that if a dangerous secret—one concerning an individual in emotional jeopardy—is held in our home, the boundaries between family and the rest of the world become rigid and impenetrable. Friends and relatives are not invited in, as Bill found: "I couldn't bring friends home, as I never knew if he would be staggering around drunk upstairs," he confessed. In such situations, "Don't tell anyone our business" becomes the family theme. The danger then is that keeping secrets may become the standard way—the only way—in which the family can relate to others.

In addition, the secret may rarely be discussed openly within the family. Bill Goldman kept his family's secret for years, long after his father's death. "Then one day I went to an AA meeting and I talked about the fact that in my family we never discussed my father's drunkenness, and I said, 'Was that unusual?' There was a huge roar of laughter from the assembled company, and somebody shouted out, 'The elephant in the living room,' referring to the fact that apparently it's common for alcoholic families not to talk about huge issues in their lives."

And anything which breaks down the ability to communicate openly in a family can be destructive. "If family members keep secrets from each other—or from the outside world—the emotional fallout can last a lifetime," suggests Imber-Black.

Being restricted from talking about something so central in your life as an alcoholic father can undermine your ability to communicate more generally with the outside world, with friends and acquaintances. You may learn to keep conversation superficial, since you feel what is truly important cannot be discussed; even where issues arise that are not connected with the secret of drinking, you fear that you may say the wrong thing.

Susan Forward, in her book *Toxic Parents,* describes the debilitating effect of the high energy required to keep the charade going. The child must always be on guard and lives in constant fear of accidentally exposing the family. To avoid that, the child often avoids making friends and thereby becomes isolated and lonely. It becomes progressively more difficult to develop personal relationships with others. The result can be a sense of alienation, isolation, and entrapment. The only way out of this dilemma is to break the rules of family secrecy, which can feel like an act of betrayal.

In the case of alcoholism, because their first and most important relationship taught them that the people they love will hurt them and be terrifyingly unpredictable, most adult children of alcoholics are terrified of becoming close to another person, proposes Susan Forward. Secrets of this nature can therefore freeze a young person's development at crucial points in life, preventing the growth of self and identity. She suggests that successful adult relationships, whether with lovers or friends, require a significant degree of vulnerability, trust, and openness—the very elements that an alcoholic household destroys. As a result, many adult children of alcoholics are drawn to people who are emotionally unavailable because of deep conflicts of their own. In this way the adult child can create an illusion of a relationship without confronting his or her terror of true intimacy.

She also claims that having to playact the charade of a normal family is damaging because it forces children to deny their own feelings and perceptions, and she underlines the difficulty for them in developing a strong sense of self-confidence if they must constantly lie about what they are thinking and feeling. Their guilt about keeping secrets makes them wonder whether people believe them. When they grow older, this sense that people doubt them can continue, causing them to shy away from revealing anything of themselves or venturing an opinion.

Bill has dealt with this problem by attempting to banish from his adult life even the normal forms of social duplicity. "I don't think I change for anybody. As a result of having to keep this terrible secret for so long, I think anybody who meets me, anywhere in the world, meets the same person, whoever that is. It is very important to me to be that, because I lived in a world of such bullshit growing up, and such continual and endless lying. It was so horrible not to be able to talk about my father's drinking. As I've gotten older and can talk with some ease about the fact that I'm the child of an alcoholic, I feel a great sense of relief."

But a secret does not have to be of such an extreme nature to have a similar psychological outcome. Bill's story underlines the fact that, if our mother drew us, as children, into keeping a family secret we may suffer as adults from some of the emotional fallout of coping with the strain. Once we have recognized that we were maneuvered by our mother into a conspiracy of silence and understood the damage it may have caused us, the crucial thing is to ensure that she is not perpetuating the situation—either by expecting you to continue to keep a family secret in this way or, if your mother is no longer alive, ensuring that her presence in your mind does not lead you to institute similar conspiracies in your family.

When She Does Things Behind Your Back

At an early age, we can encounter the shock of realizing that our mother can keep us from important information, and that things can happen behind our back.

When Lauren Hutton was almost six, her mother remarried, and they moved to start a new life in Florida. Her mother took her for her first day at her new school. At that time her name was Mary Lauren.

"I remember my first day in the new school in Florida. I guess I was in second grade. My mother took me into the classroom, then stayed standing near the teacher while the teacher started reading the roll. She called out 'Mary Hall' but I didn't even know this name. I was thinking it was vaguely interesting there was another Mary in the class, but mostly I was just looking out of the window. Then the teacher kept saying the name over, louder and louder. I looked up to see what she was yelling about, and she was staring right at me. I figured it out when I saw my mother sort of look down, embarrassed or something. I said, 'My name is not Mary Hall, my name is Mary Lauren

Hutton.' I saw my mother sneaking out toward the door, and heard the teacher say, 'No, your name is Mary Lauren Hall,' and the whole class was laughing, including the teacher. It was very, very scary. My mother had altered her own and my name to her new husband's. I felt she had taken away my identity without telling me."

We expect that our mother will be loyal to us and come to us first to consult us on important matters that concern us. The notion that our mother could go behind our back on an issue so important, so intimate, can be very disturbing.

Perhaps Lauren's mother was afraid that her little girl would rebel against changing her name from her father's to her new stepfather's, so she avoided telling Lauren about it until it was a fait accompli. In our relationship with our mother today, it may be that keeping secrets emerges in a milder form in a similar way, in which she may sometimes try to engineer the circumstances she wants before we can object. For example, if she wants us to bring our family to her house for Christmas but is afraid we may decline, she may go ahead with the preparations without consulting us, so that when we realize what she is doing, she can say, "Oh, but it's too late to change the arrangements now, I've bought everything." It is a hiding of information through fear of our preventing something happening.

Sometimes our mothers can change, but simply wishing she would change will not help. It often makes such change easier if we first of all alter the way we think about her and recognize her for her own personality and characteristics. If we have clear insight into our mother, which is consistent with the way she behaves, when she does something we do not like we can spend less time feeling shocked, upset, and betrayed. Knowing that it is just the way she is means we can then tackle her about it: "Mother, I know you like to try to organize things without telling me in advance, but I'm not going along with this one." Surprisingly often, our mother does not really realize that this is the way she habitually behaves. If we change our beliefs about our mother to recognize the way she behaves, she may begin to realize it herself.

Having Someone to Talk To

Sometimes the problems surrounding our mother's keeping of secrets are not to do with hiding information but rather to do with not discussing worrying situations. As a result, they become taboo subjects and thereby cause even more anxiety.

Jane Bedford's life changed when she was ten years old. Her father suffered a stroke, and they had to move. "We moved into a smaller house," she explained. "And then he tried one or two jobs that he thought he might be able to do, in different parts of the country." Moving homes became so frequent that Jane ended up attending about nine different primary schools. "It was a very uncertain time. I think it must have been very hard for my mother, with children and no money, and him battling to do work but not really being up to it."

"I think I was quite bright, but I wasn't told what the family problems actually were," she explained. "I knew there were many anxieties about my father's health, about money, about the future, but because these things weren't discussed I became full of anxiety and despair. I didn't know if my father was going to live or die. My mother often had migraines and would go to bed for two or three days. I suffered from fear that the whole thing was going to capsize and sink, that we were not somehow going to survive."

Jane became stressed trying to understand what was going on. "I was very, very anxious, but I had no words for this feeling. I used to be filled with an absolutely overwhelming feeling of terror. So I would try to put a story to it to explain this unknown fear to myself, and think, 'Well, I'm scared of dying!' or 'I'm afraid of failing' or 'I'm afraid of . . .'—you know. I would just try and make something to fit the feelings. Looking back, I can see what a difference it would have made if there had been someone I could have talked to."

In their book *Life and How to Survive It,* Robin Skynner and John Cleese describe research in which families judged on various criteria to be exceptionally healthy psychologically were found to discuss matters of importance openly. The parents took a clear position of authority, but the children were always consulted fully—even the youngest one—before the parents took a decision. As she can see in retrospect, it would have been helpful to Jane if her parents had communicated with her more openly in this way. Instead, seeking to protect her from their anxieties, they did not discuss their worries in front of her. The effect was to make Jane more anxious. How many mothers have made this understandable mistake?

If you had a disturbing subject in your family that your mother did not discuss with you and which still feels painful or causes you anxiety, it may help to discuss it with your mother now. Sometimes, the mere fact that something was not talked about is what made it disturbing. Hearing from your mother now about the situation then might clarify for you a set of circumstances—and they might even have been fairly straightforward—that had built up in your mind. Doing so may relieve some of the residual anxiety you have carried with you for all those years. Equally, it may help your mother to be able to talk the subject through. It could have been, as seems likely in Jane's case, that she would not talk through the issue as it caused her great anxiety and she did not want to burden you with her worry. It might be healing for her now to relive with you difficult circumstances of the past. She may even have regretted not discussing it with you at the time. To share it now might prove to be an opportunity to clear up the whole issue to your mutual benefit.

Secrets You Wish You Didn't Know

"I know my mother kept secrets," Jean Gregory said grimly. "Five years ago I was informed, to my mother's devastation, that my father had decided it was time to come clean about the family secret they had been keeping from me for my whole life. They never asked me if I thought it would be a good idea, never gave me a choice. The secret was that my mother had become pregnant with me before my parents were married, so they tried to abort me, and the abortion didn't take." Jean also believes that her mother had not wanted to tell her. "And if she had, she would never have gone about doing it the way that it was done," she said. The revelation had severe effects. "I needed two days' worth of therapy with the two of them. My mother was sobbing the whole time in the therapist's office, even though she doesn't usually cry very much. I don't think I really ever needed to know. It devastated me."

After the initial shock had worn off, Jean tried to cope with the hurtful information by trying to imagine the situation when she was conceived, so as to try to empathize with her mother. "I felt for my mother as a woman rather than as my mother," she said. "I saw her in 1961, pregnant, without the options available to a single parent today. She was twenty-four, a great beauty, and she had been proposed to countless times. My dad didn't want to marry her. He gave her money and said, 'You take care of it.'"

But there was also a second secret. "When the abortion failed, he said, 'Now I have to marry you.' So I found out that my parents never really loved each other, and yet they stayed together for twenty-something years." All, Jean believes, because of her.

One consequence of the revelations for Jean is that now, one of the things she most dislikes is when she thinks people are keeping her in the dark. "I don't like feeling I don't know the whole story, which is what I now realize was going on through the whole of my childhood."

If your mother disclosed information which had been kept from you, and you wish you had never been told, you can be left feeling deeply distrustful of people. It may undermine your ability to deal with others by engendering in you suspicions that something important in a relationship is being concealed or a need to protect yourself from others' discovering secrets about you.

In dealing with such an experience with our mother, it is best, as always, to think through the incident. If we can see things from our mother's perspective, it often helps to know exactly what it is that needs healing between us. There are many possible reasons why our mother might eventually tell us something that has formerly been a secret.

She may decide to do so out of a feeling that to tell what has been hidden will automatically be a healing process for her child. It has become the fashion in recent years to be generally more open in relationships, as I have seen in my therapeutic practice. Social expectations of no secrets can make us think that we are doing the right thing in revealing personal information, when in fact we may be abrogating our responsibility to make discriminating decisions. Nevertheless, in some cases, a mother's revelation of what has been kept secret can be enormously beneficial to her children. But deciding whether the secret should be revealed needs to be dealt with sensitively. In Jean's case, it might have been best for the story of her birth to have remained a secret. There is no apparent way the disclosure could have helped her, and the information proved to be too disturbing. It is sometimes better that there are things we do not know. But in thinking through your own experience, you should consider the fact that it is possible your mother wanted to tell you because she genuinely believed it would be good for you to know.

There may be other reasons for revealing secrets. A mother may decide to reveal information in order to relieve herself of the burden of keeping it secret. This can be dangerously self-serving. A mother should think carefully about her motives and avoid doing so simply in order to relieve her own guilt or anxiety. If you feel that your mother kept a secret from you and then later selfishly unburdened herself, it may help to discuss it with her. The information, once revealed, cannot be taken back, but the emotional impact of it, then and now, on you may be healed by sharing your hurt. Your mother may not realize she caused you distress through her actions; or she may have known but later repressed that knowledge. Being able to talk about it with her could be cathartic for you and release some of the resentment that may have accumulated over the years. In encouraging your mother to think through painful experiences like this, it is important that you broach this subject without *blaming* her. If you feel the need for recriminations, it is best to wait until you have thought the matter through carefully.

It is understandable if you do not yet feel able to talk to her about the incident. If she is sensitive about it you will need to raise the issue with her in a manner that allays her fear of immediate recriminations. She may be at fault for making the wrong decision to tell you, but her motive may have been positive. But if she revealed the secret mainly to unburden herself, she may feel guilty, and you will need to enable her to acknowledge this to herself and to you, rather than being defensive about it.

Keeping Death a Secret

As we have seen, some secrets are not really secrets as such, in that they are not hidden, but they can have a similar impact. These are events, circumstances, or aspects of life that are generally known about in a family but are never discussed: taboos. When someone dies in a family, their death often becomes a taboo subject.

I once treated a young boy whose mother had died and whose father had remarried. The boy had been upset, and, as he was causing problems at home, had been brought into the clinic. During our sessions, the boy told me that he was not allowed to talk about his mother at home. And he did not talk about her with me; although he talked about other members of his family, he never mentioned his mother. I would often ponder what he might be missing or thinking about her, and I felt he needed a chance to think about his mother actively. So in our conversations I began to talk about how mothers seemed to get left out of our conversation, and the fact I was a woman old enough to be a mother. I did not think he would be able to talk out loud about his mother, but I hoped that my interventions gave him a chance to talk internally, with himself, about her.

The boy was artistically gifted, and in our sessions he often painted. One day he did a watercolor painting of a beautiful flower and presented it to me as he left at the end of the session. I was surprised by this gesture, because he was not an emotionally expressive boy and had never done anything like it before. Then I happened to look at the calendar. The coming Sunday was Mother's Day. It dawned on me that he had given me the flower painting because I had allowed him to think about his mother. Perhaps, in a way, he thought about *me* as his mother.

This story is an example of how important it can be to have an outlet for talking about the distress of losing a loved one. If you lost your mother as a child but were forbidden to talk about it, perhaps in the belief that this would help you to get over her death more quickly, it is important to check that you are not still blocking your need to discuss and release your grief. Think through what happened, and whether you found alternative outlets for your grief. If the matter still feels painful, it may be helpful for you to talk about your mother's death now, even after all these years. The event is in the past, but your daily experience of her loss is now. Talking it out can release some of the pent-up sadness and distress.

It is quite common to repeat mistakes in our adult lives that were made with us when we were children, and it is important to be careful not to perpetuate the mistake. As a psychotherapist, I have seen how readily long-term depression can set in when a family death is repressed. So even though a death in the family is painful to talk about, it is healthier to deal with the event openly, as the examples in this chapter show. Talking about death with children does not need to be complicated, loaded with the complexities of adult concerns. Children do not need explicit details, but usually can be helped by a simple explanation and the chance to ask a few questions.

In discussing such matters from the past with our mother, it is natural that we focus on our own concerns and painful memories. We may think that to be able to talk openly about them with our mother will clear the air, making us feel better and so making possible a better relationship with our mother. But it is also important to consider what the effect of not discussing it, and not dealing with all the emotion, was on our mother, as well as the effect on ourself and the rest of the family. It can take more energy to keep something like that locked up and contained than to discuss it openly. Consider whether you would feel better if you could open the subject up with your mother. And you may find that it will be a tremendous relief for her to be able to talk about it too.

The Hidden Suicide

Sometimes a death in the family is also a secret. One day, when Becky Shearer was about ten years old, she overheard her mother talking on the telephone to a friend, and using the words "my stepmother." Becky did not know who she was referring to, as both her mother's parents were alive, and she knew of no "stepmother" in the family history. "When she got off the phone I said, 'What are you talking about, your *stepmother*?'"

Reluctantly, her mother explained to Becky that her beloved Grandma Helen was in fact her stepgrandmother, and her mother's stepmother. Her mother's own mother had committed suicide many years before. "It was such a shocking thing to me. Up until that point I had no awareness that my mother's mother had killed herself. My mother had carried the information all through her adult life, and I couldn't understand why she hadn't told me, and why it was like some big deep dark secret. I remember being really confused."

Becky's experience of discovering this secret—and this is one of the ways secrets can damage us—created a rift with her mother, a "trust gap." She felt left out and misled.

To make matters worse, her mother accused her of eavesdropping. Although in Becky's case she accidentally overheard her mother speaking about her stepmother, sometimes suspecting that important information is being withheld from us encourages us to violate another's privacy to try to discover more. We may indeed be tempted to eavesdrop on conversations, which can further corrode the trust between ourselves and our mother.

Keeping a death in the family hidden is indeed a dark secret. If your mother did this, there must be a serious reason for her to feel that it was necessary. But the discovery of such a secret can be shocking, and the distrust it creates may still adversely affect your relationship with your mother many years later. As with most issues that have lain unresolved, it is often helpful to raise the matter of the secret with your mother now. However, in talking with her about it, it may be best to focus on why she kept the secret.

In Becky's case, it turned out that her mother was herself having difficulty in dealing with the knowledge that her own mother had committed suicide, especially as Becky's mother had had a number of episodes of psychological illness. Therefore she might have avoided telling her daughter about the suicide because it might have stirred up her own concerns too much; she may have been unconsciously protecting herself from the fear that she may have inherited a tendency to suicide.

Often it is not until we grow into adulthood that we can appreciate the complex reality of our mother's own emotional life. Even then we sometimes find it hard to come to terms with it. Our mother's relationship with us has a strong grip on our psyche, and this is paramount to us, even when we know intellectually that our mother had influences on her life other than our needs and concerns. Realizing this, not just in our mind but in our emotional self, is an important part of improving our relationship with our mother.

Absent Fathers

For the growing number of us whose father was partly or wholly absent from our childhood years, there is an enormous amount missing from our experience of life. And our mother may have knowledge of that which affects our understanding of ourselves, our personal heritage and our inherited characteristics. But some mothers forbid their children to discuss their absent father.

When she was a baby, Lauren Hutton's parents separated and then divorced. Lauren cannot remember ever meeting him. "I never met my father. But my mother always said to me, 'Of course you met him, darling, of course you met him.' Evidently he had come to see me when I was fourteen months old." Some years later, when Lauren was twelve, her estranged father died. "My mother didn't tell me he had died until a year later. I was thirteen when I found out."

Although Lauren has no direct memories of her father, she felt a connection with him, a kind of presence. When information about her absent father was concealed by her mother, her feelings for him seemed devalued and she was robbed of even the tenuous connection she had with that part of her life. Lauren would have liked to have been told properly at the time that her father had died.

In coming to terms with her mother's withholding of this important information, Lauren has, as an adult, made allowances for her mother, who had at the time a volatile and difficult emotional life: "Back then she reminded me of a beautiful, original, sparkling Venetian crystal goblet that was so impossible. I imagined it was my job to hold it together."

All families go through significant changes when children are born into the family, or people join the family by marriage or other committed relationship; equally important are the changes that take place when people leave the family through separation, divorce, or death. To accommodate such changes, all family members make subtle adjustments to the way they behave. But if a secret becomes fixed in the midst of such events, the complex process of successful change is paralyzed. The effect of Lauren's mother keeping news of her father's death from her was that Lauren could not adjust properly to her new family circumstances.

Jay Epstein had a similar experience of his mother denying him information about his father. He has a different father from his brothers and sisters. His mother has been married three times, and he was conceived between the second and third marriages. His mother always concealed the identity of his biological father. Jay had assumed that his little brother's father was also his own, but as he got older, he began to suspect that something was amiss. "I didn't look anything like him, and my little brother did. I looked more like my elder brother and sister, so I started to think their dad was my dad. But by the time I was fifteen I was convinced he wasn't my dad either. I didn't want to ask my mom directly about it, so I told her I needed my birth certificate for something at school."

His mother seemed agitated about producing it. Jay can remember her playing for time, claiming that the document had not come through yet and saying things like, "'Why do these things take so long? I'm going to have to go again to the department of whatever . . .'" Five years later she gave Jay the document and admitted that the delay in producing the birth certificate had been because, when he had asked for it, she decided to have his name legally changed on the certificate to his stepfather's name.

Jay found out the secret from a cousin in New York.

They were taking the drug Ecstasy together; for him it was as if it was a truth serum. "I confessed to her that I was gay," Jay said. "She was the first family member I told. She said, 'I always knew.' Then she said, 'I have something to tell you that I have wanted to tell you for a long time,' and I said 'What? That my dad is not my real dad?' I told her that I already knew that. But she knew more; she told me some things she knew about my real father! I was very happy."

Jay confronted his mother about the fact that his stepfather was not his real father. "She denied it three times, demanding, 'Who told you that?'" Jay said that he was not going to reveal to his mother who had told him. "I was mad that she didn't tell me the truth when I asked her."

Eventually his mother admitted that what he was saying was true. "She wrote me a long letter explaining about her relationship with my real father, and told me his last name." She had fallen in love between marriages with a rich man. They had had a brief affair, and she had been pregnant with him before she met the man she married, who brought Jay up as if he was his own son.

His mother has lost touch with his biological father, and so Jay does not know where his father is, although he has reason to believe he is living on the East Coast of the United States. He has collected information about him. His cousin sent him a picture of his real father and said the man and Jay's mother had been "really happy." "He really loved my mom. Apparently my real dad saw me for the last time when I was two. He came from a rich family and was in the army or navy, and was prominent socially."

Jay's overwhelming wish is that someday his father will find him.

Today Jay is a striking-looking transvestite model, with long blond hair, an elegant body, and a beautifully made-up face. He makes himself up exactly the same way as his mother and hopes that by being so public a model his father might see his published image, realize the resemblance to the young woman he had once loved, and thereby recognize Jay. Perhaps he also thinks, "If I look like her, he will love me too." Losing touch with his father has condemned Jay to an eternal quest to fill this hole in his life.

If you had an experience like either Lauren's or Jay's, it might be useful to ponder your feelings about it. Is it an element of your life that has healed so that you no longer need to work on it? Or is it a wound you have repressed? Is there information you would still like to have but have been afraid to stir up? You might find that your mother is more willing to talk about it now, after the passage of time. You may also discover that your mother was not really able to deal well with the issue at the time. If you are able to understand and empathize with how she was then, it might help you to come to terms with what happened.

The Search for the Truth

Karen Phillips's father died when she was eighteen months old—too young to know him. He was killed in an accident while in New York City on business. "I still grieve for my father, whom I never knew," she said sadly. "I keep a beautiful photograph of him where I can see it from the foot of my bed. It is the only one I have of my father, mother, sister, and my-self—all of us together. I never did learn from my mother how my father died. My mother could not talk about it."

Karen did find out eventually what might have happened, but in an unfortunate manner, when she was nearly thirteen and in her first year of high school. The father of a friend, with whom she had sat in the playground every day, committed suicide by shooting himself. When her friend returned to school and they were sitting with the usual group of girls in the playground, her friend, in her anguish and grief, turned to Karen and said, "And your father threw himself under a train!" "I had no idea what she was talking about," Karen remembered. "I had never asked how my father died. I had just been told it was an accident. It was a shock to find out this way."

As an adult, Karen moved to New York expressly to find out more about the circumstances of the accident, but the official records no longer exist. "I tried, with a great deal of anguish, to find anything and everything I could. I was able to obtain a copy of the death certificate, which said 'jumped or fell,' so it could be either. I think it possibly was accidental—he could have slipped. Who would know? I read all the newspaper archives, but I could not find a newspaper account of the accident at all."

Karen's mother was traumatized by this tragic accident. "I believe that my mother has been in an emotional concrete bunker ever since," Karen said. "She never approached us in a mothering way. I think she was so afraid that if she allowed herself to put her arms around us and really hug us, and, God forbid, anything should happen, she wouldn't be armored against the loss. My belief is that she kept on armoring herself again and again. You can see her emotion is closed in, and when it does explode out of her it comes out in angry, bitter bursts. She cannot to this day smile at me, hug me. Nothing."

Karen's mother did eventually remarry—and then the tragedy of her life was compounded, for her second husband also died.

"Her way of dealing with it was to exclude us from grief and mourning again. We were not permitted, even though at fourteen and fifteen we were old enough, to go to the funeral. The aftermath of his death was hidden from us. After the funeral, I remember saying to my mother, 'What will we do now?' and she said, 'You do what you've always done. You go upstairs and brush your teeth.'"

But recently, there has been a glimmer of light in Karen's story. "On our last visit with my mother, nine months ago, she wanted to start talking about my father almost immediately, which was very strange," Karen said. Her mother began telling Barry, Karen's partner, some of the details of the accident. "It was as if by telling Barry little things, she could talk to me but not talk to me, and I understood that." Perhaps this gesture is an indication that Karen's mother is finally ready to begin to unlock some of her pent-up emotion and deal with it more openly.

If you have a death, or similar taboo in your family that has never been discussed openly, be on the alert for any signs that your mother may now be able to talk about it. She may even want to talk about it, but not know quite how to begin.

Putting the Pieces Together

In resolving issues with your mother from your shared past, it is important to be clear about what it is your right to know. If you want to ask your mother, say, for more information about a father who was missing for part or all of your childhood, and you know that this is a sensitive subject for her, it can help to acknowledge to her how difficult it may be, but also to make it clear to her that it is difficult for you, too. In trying to repair the damage caused by a secret, you need to make your mother understand how important the subject and the effects of keeping the secret are to you.

In addition, try to get your mother to fill in as much as she can; correcting not only the direct lies, but also the part she has omitted to tell you.

If you are not in frequent contact with your mother, you may be tempted to broach the subject of a secret at an occasional family gathering, such as a birthday, wedding, or retirement party. But talking about a secret needs an opportunity for concentrating on it alone, to ensure that it is not lost in the midst of other family concerns. So to help you both to handle a life-altering secret, it is important to choose an appropriate time and make specific arrangements for such a talk if necessary.

Remember that in discussing secrets with your mother, you may be in danger of hearing things you wish you had not known. You will have to take responsibility for the information she tells you. But take courage. In my experience as a psychotherapist, I have seen that, despite the risks, there nearly always comes a time when truth is best.

8 SAYING GOODBYE

The loss of our mother through death will, for many of us, be difficult, for all sorts of reasons. If we are close to her, we will miss her love terribly. If we involve her in our life, talking things over and asking her advice, we may feel lonely and without support. On the other hand, if our relationship has been difficult or downright bad, we may feel relief or guilt, sadness that we left issues unresolved, or despair that we never had the relationship we wanted. We may feel sorrow but also feel glad to be free from a tangle of obligations. We may experience only numbness—because our feelings about our mother are repressed or because we have been cut off from her altogether—as Terry O'Neill did. "I don't think I ever really grieved for my mother," he said. "I had to take over the funeral arrangements because my father felt unable to do it, and I remember trying to make jokes at the wake afterward. Only when my father died did I cry for both of them."

But although the experience of losing our mother is different for all of us, the interviews for this book revealed that as we face the prospect of losing our mother, we seem to go through several different stages. These begin with denial and unwillingness to face her eventual death; next, realization that it is going to happen; then a wish to resolve outstanding issues or rifts with her; then relief, for both selfish and unselfish reasons, at the prospect or reality of her being gone; after this, for some of us a desire to help her to come to terms with her own impending death; and finally after she has died a need to keep a connection with her of various kinds. These stages are not experienced universally and do not necessarily happen in this sequence; some people skip over various stages or experience more than one at a time. But understanding these common perspectives may help each of us to deal with this issue in our own life. Let us consider these stages in turn.

One Day She Will Die

"When my mother told me she had not been well lately and that her blood pressure is going up, I realized I'm not ready for her to die," Nicole Farhi confided.

We all know that one day we will lose our mother, but the thought is hard to accept. As a result, many of us try to deny it by pushing it out of our mind.

Intellectually Jenny Goldman knows her mother is getting older and less energetic, but emotionally she cannot accept the implications. "She is getting more physically tired. Her stamina isn't what it once was. But it's hard to imagine her gone. She looks amazing," Jenny enthused about her mother, perhaps trying to find an antidote to the thought that as her mother ages, she is getting closer to death. Jenny also has the insight to realize that her desire to see her mother as young goes beyond physical vanity and is partly about herself: "I think it's really hard to see my mother get older, because I still think of myself as frozen in time, as a teenager, and it makes me sad to grow older."

The death of our mother marks a big step forward in our own life journey. As we move one generation nearer to our own death, we are reminded of our mortality. Contemplating this is one of the hardest tasks in life, and being afraid to do so brings up many difficult feelings.

If our mother is still alive, it can be helpful to play in our mind's eye the prospect of her not being with us anymore and explore how we really feel about that. It is best to try to observe the feelings that arise—which may include regret, panic, sadness, anger, relief, euphoria, and perhaps guilt if any of our reactions seem improper to us—without judging or dismissing them. There is nothing unnatural about any of these emotions, and if we can observe them first and only then consider why we feel them, we may learn a great deal about how we really feel about our mother today; contemplating being without her clarifies emotions of which we may not normally be aware. And anticipating our possible reaction to losing her helps us to face more directly the fears about her dying that we may repress. Familiarity with these emotions often helps to reduce their unsettling effects.

Your Time Together Is Limited

One of the effects of denying to ourselves that our mother is aging is that we fall into the fallacy of believing there is no real urgency in our relationship with her. We imagine that she is always going to be there, and so there will always be time to deal with things. But if we can grasp that our time with her is limited, we can value her presence now more fully.

Sometimes it takes a dramatic event to bring about this realization. When I was a young girl, my mother was the head counselor at the summer camp where we went every year. It was great to have her there when I was little, but by the time I was thirteen and wanted to appear sophisticated and grown-up, her presence at the camp embarrassed me. So we made a pact. When we next went to the camp, she would pretend not to be my mother; even though we both had the same last name, she would say we were not related. This worked fine for the first few days, until one of the other girls in my hut said something that hurt my feelings; I went running to my mother's cabin, crying. She gently chided me: "I thought I wasn't your mother for two weeks." Through my tears I protested that the idea had been a bad one on my part, and asked if we could please change the agreement. She, of course, scooped me into her arms.

The next year I would not go at all because she was there. We had an argument about it and I would not say good-bye to her when she left for the camp. On her journey my mother fell asleep at the wheel and hit a bridge. She was in a coma for six weeks and the doctors feared she would die. She lost her left eye and was badly bruised and swollen on the left side of her face. I have always, to this day, thought that the accident was my fault because she was driving while stressed and preoccupied by our argument. But it made me appreciate my mother, and I was lucky to have this realization of her value brought home to me, for three years later she died of cancer. In the meantime I had treasured her presence more because of that realization.

As adults, we need to remember that our mother is growing older and that she will not be here forever. We should make the most of our time with her now, whether by enjoying a good relationship or improving a bad one. In previous chapters we have considered some of the many struggles we may have in our relationship with our mother, problems whose causes sometimes originated decades ago. The past is also very relevant to saying good-bye to our mother, for our mother's death will end the longest relationship we have had with anyone. In dealing with this process, outright sentimentality can be a strength. It can help to allow feelings of nostalgia to override some of our adult rationality, to appreciate just what we will be losing. To do this, it helps if we consciously hold our mother's best qualities in our mind.

Our relationship with our mother may be difficult, but that does not mean that we will not miss her. "My mother often says that I am her best friend," Monica Benton said. "It feels like a bit of a burden, because I wouldn't say she was mine. I love her, but she irritates me quite a lot, and is sort of losing her marbles now. In fact, she drives me crazy. But life without her is the most appalling thought. Just the void without her would be . . ." Her voice trailed away. "She permeates our whole family with her presence." For many of us, as our mother ages she may become vague, or irritable, or forgetful or self-centered— all of which will make her hard work to be with. But, as Monica says, it is likely that we are so used to our mother's presence that being without it will be a shock. Realizing this makes it easier to put up with the irritations she brings to us now, and to enjoy the time we spend with her despite them.

We need to make time to enjoy our mother's presence, as Arianna Huffington realizes. Her mother has always lived near or with her daughter. "We're incredibly close," Arianna explained. "She's utterly central to my life; she's central to my children's life. She's always been very energetic, and she's the ultimate nurturer." Arianna is becoming aware that her mother, at the age of seventy-five, is beginning to slow down. "I have seen in the last two years that suddenly age has become a major factor. When she gets sick it's so much harder for her to get well. She has a blood condition, which has brought me face-to-face with her death and the fact that she won't be alive forever. But I feel that I'm still not handling well enough the fact that she's still alive—I need to make more time for her than I'm making, but it's been hard because of my work deadlines and my children."

This issue of how to give time to parents amid a busy and demanding life is a common one. Mike Pierce is wrestling with it. "I know they are getting older and things are happening to them, and all of that," he said, "and I know they want me to spend more time at the house—just to come by, cut the grass, things like that. I try to get by there as often as I can, but they live a long way away, so it's not easy. There are always excuses like, 'I had to work,' 'I was tired.' But time passes, and when they are not there anymore, I know I am going to say, 'Would it really have been so much for me just to go over there and spend the day with them sometimes?' I struggle with that."

When we realize that our time with our mother is limited, working out how to balance the everyday pressures of life with a desire to help and spend time with our aging mother is as important for ourself as for her. If you feel anxiety about this issue, use your anxiety as a motivating strength in your resolve to spend time with your mother.

Making Up Before She Dies

Not long ago I was at a cocktail party and talking to two men in their fifties about their mothers. One man's mother had lived to an old age, and he said how wonderful it was that he had had time to make reparation with her and to heal wounds from their rifts when he was younger. But the other man's mother had died without their resolving their difficulties, and he said he had always wished that she had been alive longer so he could have done the same.

If we realize early enough the inevitability of our mother's death and that it could happen at any time, the prospect of saying good-bye can encourage us to start trying to heal issues that distance us from her. We have time now, if only we use it.

Carolyn Fulton had a difficult relationship with her mother but worked hard to improve it right to the end. "When my mother died, I was numb for a long time," she said. "There was a sense that I had been pulling on a rope, as if in a tug of war, and the person on the other end had suddenly let go. With the struggle over, I was left with the question, 'What do I do with this empty space?'" But although the end of the struggle was disorienting, she was comforted by the fact that before her mother had died, they had achieved some resolution of the issues between them.

At the end of her life, her mother finally told Carolyn that she loved her. "I had been to see her when she was dying, and I'm not actually sure that she said 'I love you,' but I think she did. And of course, I said, 'Yes, I love you too, Mother.' I still have a hard time trusting that she said it, but I think she did."

We need to remember that saying good-bye is something our mother is facing also, and we may be able to help her to do and say things that have been too difficult for her before. A declaration of love at the end, for instance, as in Carolyn's case, is better than none at all. Whatever the issues that remain unresolved between us, if we think there is a chance for such an important healing connection, even a small chance, we should keep on trying; it finally worked for Carolyn, and may for us.

Relief When She Dies

"I think it would be a huge relief," Kathleen Jackson said, when asked how she thought she would cope with her mother's death. "I would be free. For years, the guilt and the resentment that I feel toward her have taken so much energy out of me. Then I feel wicked when I hear myself say that. I wish I could get to a point where I can accept that good and bad things had to happen, and that's human life. Then there could come a level of acceptance. I've been frustrated that I haven't achieved that. I seem to have worked so hard on it for so long."

Sometimes relief comes in surprising circumstances: even a good relationship makes its own demands. Terry Jones was so close to his mother that he sometimes felt, "How could the love I feel for anybody else match up to the love I have for my mom? In a way it was very difficult for me to believe that I could love anybody else." When she died, he said, "There was a certain relief in a way, which is stupid considering how much I loved her. I miss her, as I loved her so much, but I suddenly felt I was free to look at life in my own terms, not just at how I could make things better for Mom, and free to love other people."

Terry's feelings illustrate that sometimes we can love our mother so much that it becomes a burden; yet we only realize this when she dies and we feel a sense of relief. This and Kathleen's story remind us that emotions are complex and sometimes seem contradictory, but they are still perfectly natural. In exploring emotions of relief for what they can tell us about our relationship with our mother, we should not feel obliged to make them all fit into a neat pattern or feel guilty for feeling them.

Many of the interviewees talked of the relief they would feel or did feel at their mother's death, for various reasons.

Toward the end of her life, Michael Winner's mother's excessive gambling became an addiction. She lost £7 million at the Cannes casino in the 1970s, selling antiques and paintings in order to meet her debts. They were meant to be left to him. In a desperate attempt to get further money for her gambling, she went through eleven firms of solicitors in the hope of suing him for more money, but no law firm would do this as he had done nothing wrong. "You could say the relationship was over-emotional," said Michael.

"I remember once, when I went to see her, I rang the doorbell of her hotel room and there was no answer, so I got the maid to open the door. She let me go in. My mother had not been well for many years. She had hung on as far as the age of seventy-eight, and she was getting closer to dying with each week. I opened the door and she was lying on the floor, naked. She had collapsed and was obviously not in a good way. For a fleeting second I thought to myself, 'All my troubles would be over if I just closed the door and walked away.' But of course I couldn't do that, so I rang the doctor, who later said to me, 'If you had not called when you did your mother would have died.' I thought it was a terrible thing that, even for a second, that thought had crossed my mind, but I have to say that when she eventually did die, my first thought was, 'Thank God it's over.'"

But Michael is able to see her in a broader perspective than just his experience of the last few very difficult years.

"I miss her. No question. I think of her a great deal. I think of her positive qualities as well as her minuses, and I love her. And I think above all with great sadness that she did not create a happy life for herself. For her the glass was always half-empty rather than half-full. I think, 'Was there anything I could have done or should have done?' But there really wasn't."

If your mother has or had problems of such severity that they profoundly affected you—for instance, causing you to feel rejected—it is understandable if you feel nothing but resentment and relief when she has died. But these are emotions that can cut you off from your mother. If, despite the problems between you, you can manage to feel some compassion for her, as Michael can, when she dies, although you may still feel relieved, you will keep your connection with her; and retaining her presence in your life in this way will give you the chance to heal within you some of the rifts you have had with her, even though she is gone.

Helping Her to Die

The responsibility of playing an active part in helping our mother to come to terms with her own aging and death is a stage that is often hard for young adults to understand—as I discovered when I met my present husband, when I was about forty and my elder son was nineteen. When I realized how serious the relationship was, I decided to tell my son about it. I wanted to make sure that he understood that he would not be left out, and it would relieve a little of his worry about me. I took him out to lunch and said, "Honey, I just want you to know that, after coping on my own for twenty years, I'm now with someone who I want to marry. It will be such a relief for you because you won't have to worry about me in my old age." He said, "Mother, I've never thought about it." I had been projecting on to him worries that he hadn't even imagined.

With maturity, however, when we understand more about the process of aging ourselves, looking after our mother as she nears death can be an important stage of saying good-bye. One of my friends in Texas was an only child and depended on her mother in a childlike way until her mother became ill in her eighties. I was astounded then when she chose to have her mother die at home. It was beautiful to watch my friend growing stronger as a person, as, slowly and painfully, she went through the process of saying good-bye to her mother. The experience of playing an active role in her mother's death was enriching for her, and I do not believe she could have developed in this way without it.

Mothers sometimes have strong feelings about how and where they want to die. Once, on my way to JFK airport, I began chatting with the cabdriver. After graduating from college in Haiti, he told me, he became a political journalist and was very against the Duvalier regime, which made his safety uncertain. His mother managed to scrape together the money to smuggle him out to New York City, where he gained American citizenship. He did not go back to journalism, because he could make more money from driving, and he soon saved enough to bring the rest of his family over to join him in America. But when the time came, his mother refused to come, even though her life was in danger because of his escape. She said that despite this, her life lay in Haiti and she could not see herself dying in another country. This man had to accept her wishes, for part of taking responsibility for our mother's death is having the strength to be aware of what *she* wants and not be distracted by our own needs.

In some cases, this awareness includes her knowing when she is ready to die. "In the last few months of her life my mother was getting frail, depending on people in a way she had never wanted to before," Michael Palin said. "While I was in Switzerland with the family on a skiing holiday, someone rang up and said, 'I think your mother is fading fast and may not last out the week—could you come back?' I felt that she was waiting for me to come back, so I went. I felt absolutely right being there with her, but there was no question of my saying, 'You must stay alive.' I could tell that she was ready to die, knew she was going to die and was happy to die, as far as one can say that about anybody. After she died, I felt shock, and then gradually a sense of her absence and loss, but those feelings have always been tempered by my sense that she felt it was the right time to die."

Responsibility in your mother's dying, then, is about listening to your mother and trying to be aware of how, where, and when she would like to die when the time comes. To reach this stage you need to be able to transcend your own anxieties about her death—another example of how managing your mother is largely about managing yourself.

Sometimes, helping our mother to die can entail our presence to the very end. Helena Bonham Carter described how her mother helped *her* mother, Helena's grandmother, to die. "Granny was a very vivid figure. Even though she was quite old, she always looked much younger than her age, and was always very fit. She was a painter, and just last year she had a solo exhibition. Mom's brother had moved to the States, so toward the end the emotional looking after of Granny, having her for holidays and weekends, fell on Mom's shoulders. It meant we saw her quite often. But in the last four months she became quite deaf, and we could see her declining physically. Then Granny wrote her autobiography and finished it three days before she died. She must have known that something was going to happen; we found out after she died that only two weeks previously she had checked that her arrangements with the cemetery were in order.

"The night before she died, she and Mom had gone to the theater. Mom said to her, 'You look tired,' and she said, 'Yes, I'm very tired.' The next day she rang my mom and said, 'I think I'm dying—you had better come.' Mom went to her and saw that she was failing, so she put her to bed. Granny was still conscious. Mom lay next to her on the bed. She told me later, 'I just kept telling her that she looked good, and that she was dying with style, and that I loved her.' It took about three hours for her to slowly drift off. There then came a point where my mom thought Granny might rally, and the doctor, who was there, said, in her earshot, 'We'll take her to the hospital'—and Granny just died. She didn't want to go to the hospital. It was a perfect death, really.

"Afterward, Mom was very emphatic that all the family should see Granny. I went up to see the body, and it was good: there was nothing macabre about it. In fact, it was a rather beautiful experience."

A Continuing Connection with Her

It is important to realize that, in a sense, our mother never leaves us; she will stay with us emotionally for the rest of our life, even though she has died. When our mother dies, while it is too late to discuss, confront, or renegotiate issues with her directly, it is never too late to think them through by ourselves, to deepen our understanding and perhaps gain insights into our relationship. In the light of these we may feel able to revise in our mind, and then in our heart, feelings about many issues pertaining to her. In a mysterious way, although she has gone, we can still improve our relationship with her.

Sometimes there are practical ways of helping us, before or after her death, to maintain that continuing connection with our mother.

Such arrangements can help her and us to come to terms with saying good-bye to each other. "I have told my mother what her monument to immortality will be," David Jones explained. "At the end of our house in Somerset, England, we have an area that was the old cider house, joined on to the main house. The plan is to turn it into a library that, because the area is two stories, will have a gallery at the top. We will spend whatever money she leaves me on that, and I am going to have a plaque somewhere, to my mother's memory. She thinks it is a good idea, because it reflects her lifelong enthusiasm for education." David's mother was able to enjoy the knowledge that he wished to keep a connection with her after she was gone and that he cared enough to have gone to the trouble of planning it.

John Goldwyn had a difficult relationship with his mother when he was growing up, but had worked at it and improved it in later life. After she had died, John had the opportunity to purchase her house. "My wife said to me, 'Shall we buy this house?' and I looked at it and said, 'Well, I don't know—it wasn't the happiest place I've lived in.' And Colleen said, 'She would want you to have this house.' So I restored the house to the way it was when she bought it. It is a happy place now, a very happy place."

When Daniel Abraham's mother died of cancer, he did not grieve much for her: "I didn't feel much of anything. I still don't." But he carries out a little ceremony. "There is a Jewish tradition that you go and visit the grave, and put a stone on it. I do that irregularly. When I put the stone on my father's grave, I miss him. When I put the stone on my mother's grave, I think, 'That's that!'" Although Daniel's feelings for his mother were not as strong as those he had for his father, this ritual helps to maintain a connection with her.

Sometimes we maintain a connection without even being aware of it. All my life, I have loved white flowers, and I have filled my gardens and my house with them. Recently one of my friends, Ann Hatch, died. In my opinion, she was a wonderful wife and mother. Every year she and her husband, David, used to have a party in their old converted windmill and this year David would host the party alone. As my husband and I were getting ready to leave for the party, I decided to take David some flowers from the garden. We had just moved house, and of course the people from whom we bought the house did not have my usual embargo on colored flowers. In the garden I saw the most beautiful red roses. I went to cut some, but found I could not. Suddenly, I realized why.

Where I grew up, in Oklahoma, on Mother's Day all the children wore a flower: a red one if your mother was alive and a white one if she was dead. After my mother died, when I was only sixteen, I remember feeling like a freak arriving at the church and being the only child with a white flower. By growing only white flowers, it was as if for thirty-nine years I had carried on the custom; I grew them because I liked them better, without realizing the real reason.

As I looked at the roses, I saw that red stood for the forces of life and the coursing of the blood through our veins. I wanted my friend Ann's memory to *live*, and so I picked red roses, for the first time since my mother had died all those years ago. Now, when I replant our new garden, I am sure I will add red roses.

This seems more appropriate to me now, for my mother lives on inside me. I do not think of her every day, but I know she is always at the back of my mind for me to call on when I am lonely, sad, or ill. I also think of her at special times, such as when I experience joy in my children or achieve something to be proud of in my work. In that sense, I have not said good-bye to her at all.

9

TEN STEPS TOWARD A BETTER RELATIONSHIP WITH YOUR MOTHER

Learning to better manage

our relationship with our mother can be a big

project which, like most big projects, is best tack-

led in smaller steps. In this last chapter we review

ten steps, as described to us by the people we interviewed, that had been effective in improving their relationships with their mothers. They are not necessarily surprising, or revolutionary, or presented in any particular order of importance, but they have worked for many people. Try them.

Remember Your Mother's Age

One of my best friends always closes the door, no matter where we are, and is uncomfortable until he has done so. One day I said to him, "Why are you always closing doors?" He laughed and said, "Because my mother might walk in." Of course, the mother he was referring to is the internalized one, whom we knew as children and who lives in our imaginations. She is not the same mother we deal with today. Our mothers have changed.

In this book there are many examples of how our mother changes and what we can do to cope with those changes. Yet there is a factor that we often disregard, because it seems to us simple, and perhaps too obvious to merit consideration: their age. As children, we often do not think of our mother as having an age. Age, we think then, is a characteristic of an old person. It is not until later, when we become conscious of our mother as an individual adult, that her age enters our awareness. Even so, for many of us, it does not alter our view of her; she is still, primarily, our mother. Becoming aware of our mother's age, not just in numbers of years, but in terms of her psychological and physical state, often helps us to understand her better, which strengthens our relationship.

Even if our mother is relatively young—perhaps only in

her thirties—she grew up a generation earlier than us. She has probably lived her formative years in a social environment in which attitudes toward matters such as divorce, abortion, higher education, unemployment, and working mothers were all different from those we have experienced. Her values may seem old-fashioned, but all the influences she had from her parents and peers have had an impact on the way she evolved as a person. No matter how much she adapts to the changing world, there are experiences from earlier in her life that will remain with her forever.

Roberta Farmer's mother harbored a secret for many years. "Eventually she told me what it was: that as a young woman, she had had an abortion. This was before she had me, and my parents weren't married at the time. She felt awful about it, because she really wanted a baby, but felt it would be wrong to have it." When Roberta heard this revelation, she felt an overwhelming sense of empathy with her mother, and understanding of her point of view. Secrets such as this remind us not only of the acutely wounding nature of some life experiences, but also the changing context of social disapproval. Thirty or forty years ago, it was not only socially unacceptable for a woman to have an abortion, but also illegal in many states.

Sometimes we become impatient with our mother because she does not agree with us about various matters. But we need to remember that it is unreasonable to expect her to change totally from the way she was brought up. If we imagine what it must have been like to grow up in her generation, we can understand her behavior then and now. It can be helpful, too, to let her know that we are aware of this, perhaps by encouraging her to tell us about what things were like when she was young. My husband's mother, Muriel, is one hundred years old, and before we met he had not asked her about the stories of her childhood. Now he has, and we have both learned so much about her from these tales and understand her better for it.

Muriel has always been amused at how rebellious her son is in the face of authority and the expected norms of behavior. Yet when we discovered more about her early life, before John was born, we saw that she too bucked authority. She had grown up in a strict Victorian family atmosphere. In the 1920s, when she was a young woman, she fell in love. But her family, and in particular her father, were displeased because Reg, the handsome man of her choice, was not "proper" enough. He was a bit of a free spirit. He had served in the merchant marines and really enjoyed his life of freedom and travel. Muriel Cleese always tells of his wonderful sense of humor and love of fun. But her family would not relent in their disapproval of him, and so she and Reg often met on the sly. When he proposed marriage, Muriel decided to take a strong stand against her family. Each time she left home to see him secretly, she would take some of her trousseau in her handbag for Reg to take, until eventually she had moved enough to get by in another home. They then ran away and got married. Her father did not speak to her for two years. Being snubbed by him (and by her sisters, although her mother was sympathetic) upset her terribly because she had been very close to them all. The young couple moved to London. In the end, Muriel's mother arranged with Reg for the whole family to meet for tea in a London hotel, and the rift was resolved. Understanding Muriel's resolve in bucking the family's disapproval and the mores of the time helped us to know her more fully as a person, rather than only in her role as John's mother.

As our mother gets older, we have to deal with the effects of her aging. However, we need to be careful not to overreact by going from being relatively unaware of her age to the other extreme of seeing her as old, with all the restrictions that that implies. I am a grandmother in my midfifties. Recently I went to visit my younger son, who at the time was living in the rain forest in Mauritius. Although I am physically very active, if Clinton had asked me beforehand whether I wanted an exhausting adventure, I would surely have declined out of a natural reluctance to place myself under such stress. As it was, because he was so keen to show me what he had been doing, I was swept up by his enthusiasm.

I found the conditions there to be very primitive and challenging but managed to survive. Until, that is, my son asked me to join him in climbing a very tall tree in which Gerald Durrell, the famous zoologist, had had his epiphany about saving animals from extinction. I stood rooted to the ground in the pouring rain, staring up into broad branches of the tree, feeling a rising sense of panic. I heard from Clinton the very same remarks that I had heard myself saying to him all his young life: "It's an important step in your development"; "It's a chance of a lifetime"; "You have to push yourself to gain strength." His final remark was, "I'll be right behind you!"—as though this would have helped if we both crashed to the floor of the forest, hours from civilization! Well, I did not want to let him down. I do not want to do it again, but I did it, terrified and drenched in sweat all the way up and down. It is an experience I will never forget.

Our mother may seem old to us, but new experiences can still be important to her. While we need to be aware of our mother's age, it does not necessarily mean that she can no longer do things that are physically challenging.

Of course, when our mother gets very old we might not expect her to have the physical strength of younger women, but she may still have a lot of psychological vitality. Nancy Bresse's mother is almost eighty. "She's a very passionate person. She's an artist—she does oils. Also, she's just started her third manuscript: she is writing a book about New Mexico." We need to be careful not to underestimate our mother's need for stimulation, and not lower our expectations of her capabilities in this regard just because we see her aging physically. I remember our taking Muriel to the opera when she was ninety; she had never been to an opera before. She still talks about the excitement of doing something new and about entering the beautiful theater for the first time. Observing our mother can help us find practical ways to encourage her to live life well as long as possible.

Sometimes we are able to help our mother as she grows older by having her move in to live with us. This can have many benefits for us, including the opportunity to deepen our relationship with her. But of course, the passage of years can also mean eventually that our relationship with our mother reaches a different balance. Our mother may become much more dependent on us. Nancy, for instance, feels that in her relationship with her mother, she has become the parent and her mother the child. "It sounds terrible, but I became almost resentful about it. But then I welcome it also, for I feel protective of her."

When a reversal of roles happens, it can be psychologically difficult for us, for we are used to being the child. It is natural for us to be ambivalent about filling this highly responsible and demanding role for our mother. It is a role for which we have not been trained, and there is usually no longer a culture of extended families in which the older generation is looked after by the younger one. We should acknowledge our feelings of resentment and not feel guilty about them. It can help also to talk to other people who have mothers of about the same age and find out how they are coping.

Actuarial statistics are commonly cited to show the rapid rise in life expectancy in recent years. Even if your mother is of an advanced age, if she is in reasonable health today it is likely that she may live for some years yet. But of course, physical problems do arise eventually. We need to remember that if our mother becomes difficult to look after and needs a lot of physical as well as psychological care, she is probably aware of the problem, too. We should not be afraid to talk it over with her. She may not want to face up to the difficulties. On the other hand, I have seen many mothers who have welcomed the chance to talk out the possibilities, rather than repress them. Some mothers, for example, would rather enter assisted living centers or nursing homes than be a burden on us. Our mother has her dignity to maintain, and it is sometimes better for her, as well as for us, to remain as independent as possible.

On the other hand, if we live far away from our mother, we may feel guilty about not seeing her enough, and it can become increasingly difficult, as she ages, to feel we can help her. Nicole Farhi is in regular contact with her eighty-year-old mother, who lives in Paris. "I talk to her on the telephone from London every Saturday when she is in good health, and every two or three days when she has a problem. I feel I am dealing with her aging, but when she is not well, I feel upset that I am not near her." We can compensate for living at a distance by having our mother visit, if she is able to, but sometimes this is not quite what she wants. She may find it difficult leaving her home and routines. "I have invited her to come here to visit me, but she doesn't want to travel; she won't come here," Nicole said. "She belongs to her place. She's very busy. She plays bridge every week at a club with friends, takes care of her apartment, goes out shopping, goes out with her sisters and brothers . . . she's always busy." Even when she visits Nicole, she feels out of place and misses her routine. "She comes here every year for a month, but after two or three weeks she gets restless and feels useless."

If you live at a distance from your mother, weigh up carefully the advantages and disadvantages to your relationship. While you may wish you could see her more often, perhaps that is better achieved by arranging trips together than by trying to live close to her. Traveling gives you a chance to be together, without invading each other's territory, disrupting home routines, and so on.

While life expectancy is rising, it is also probable that your mother will die before you do. One element of realizing your mother's age is knowing that your time with her is limited. While writing this book I did a lot of flying to meet with different people I interviewed. On one of these trips someone asked me to take a quite large and breakable present from Chicago to New York. I was traveling business class, which on the smaller airplanes consists of about twenty seats. My seat was near the front, and I was one of the last passengers to board. I am not particularly tall, and I struggled to place the large package in the overhead bin. None of the male flight attendants or businessmen around me offered to help. However, from the last row of the section a handsome young man in camping gear and a straw hat walked up the aisle, took the package from me, and deftly placed the item in the bin. As I turned to say thank you, I realized it was John Kennedy, Jr. When our flight landed and I rose to remove my item, there he was again, already holding the package and offering to carry it out onto the concourse for me. We had little chance for conversation, because he was stopped frequently by fellow passengers asking if he was the real John John or something along those lines. When we reached the concourse, the press awaited him. I said thank you, and he disappeared into the crowd.

My immediate reaction, I suppose because of this book, was to write a note to his mother, Jacqueline Kennedy Onassis, to tell her what a splendid job she had done in raising such a courteous son. I now regret bitterly that I did not, but on reasoning with myself at the time, it began to seem a rather silly thing to do. She would have no idea who I was, and I was sure other people had already told her what a lovely son he was—all of the excuses were there. She died two weeks later, and the chance was gone forever.

If I could somehow teach a person how to make a mother feel wonderful, I think I would recommend that they send letters like the one I did not write. The little things we teach our children go forward without our knowledge, whether they be good or bad. How many times have you caught yourself doing something and realized you learned it from your mother?

The morning that John Kennedy went missing, I was a guest on television. At that time no one knew if he was alive or dead, but there were lots of stories of his foolishness in flying when he did. All I could think of was this tiny story, and my wish that I had told his mother of his courtesy to me. Now they are both gone.

Remember your mother's age. Say the things you want to say while you have the chance.

> You and your mother come from different generations so it is unreasonable to expect her to change totally from the way she was brought up. Statistics show that your mother may live to an old age. Expect and plan for this.

Listen to Your Mother

I remember being teased as a child because my skin tans to a deep brown. In Oklahoma in those days, racial prejudice was still strong among the white community, so if your skin was anything but white, you were teased. I remember arriving home in floods of tears and sitting in my mother's lap to be reassured that brown skin was just as beautiful as white. Thirty years later in London, I was seeing James, a little boy of three, for psychotherapy. He was one of the most beautiful children I've worked with. His father was a coal black Rastafarian, and his mother was a blue-eyed white woman. James was the color of honey. One summer's day, we were sitting together in the therapy room drawing pictures, and our bare arms were side by side. He looked up at me with concern in his big brown eyes, and said, "When will Mother be the same color as us?" Psychoanalytic theory did not seem to cover this question! I remembered the homily that my mother had given me when I was being teased all those years ago: "Pretty is as pretty does; beauty is only skin deep," and tried to interpret this principle to him in words he would understand, and this is what he needed to hear.

Generally, as we grow up we naturally tend to reject what our mother has told us. Often it sounds old-fashioned or folksy and not sophisticated enough for the world we live in today. Yet I have found as a psychotherapist and in other areas of my life that, sometimes, the things my mother told me long ago are remarkably useful. So if your mother is still offering maxims for your life, try to resist the temptation to reject automatically what she says. It can be worth trying to listen; she may well have some useful things to say.

It will still be the case, of course, that she will sometimes tell you things you disagree with, but if you can listen with an open mind, you will encourage her to open up to you more fully. Let her know that you understand her point of view. This does not mean that you have to necessarily *share* it. But if your mother knows that you respect her point of view, it will help her to feel closer to you. Even if you later explain to her how you see things, and that your views differ, the fact that you have recognized her perspective is crucially important. Once she knows this, she may be less likely to try to impress her more unwelcome ways of doing things on to you.

Hugh Hefner, founder of *Playboy* magazine, explained how "mutual listening" with his mother affected his life. He and his mother did not have the same perspectives on life, but they respected each other's views. Hugh's mother died recently, at age 101, and they had a close relationship right to the end. They had a very strong bond as mother and son, but not necessarily an intimate one. "My folks were very prudish. Mother maintained a very puritan home. There was no liquor allowed in my home, no cigarettes. No profanity. Mom did not show affection physically, and did not kiss the children, for fear it might spread germs. And when I reached adolescence, I think my interest in the things that led to *Playboy* were a reaction to the lack of showing of affection from my mother when I was a child."

Even though Hugh's mother had a different outlook from his, she still listened to him. And she helped him to start the magazine, even though she did not approve of it. "The magazine was started on no money at all. I borrowed $600 by hocking furniture and managed to raise about $8,000 in all plus some credit from a printing company. When I went to my parents in the summer of 1952 and asked them if I could borrow some money for this venture, my father declined. But my mother had been working and had some money of her own, and gave me a check for $1,000. Even though she did not believe in the magazine, she always gave me support." It is not hard to imagine the difference of opinion between Hugh and his mother. If she had not met Hugh's father, "she might have become a missionary," he said. "The conflict with my mother was always relevant throughout my life, because I never was able to fully have the satisfaction of my mother really understanding and appreciating what I had accomplished." During one conversation Hugh had with his mother, he asked her whether she was proud of him. "Oh, yes," she said. But then she turned to a third person who was with them, and said, "I'm proud of him, but I would have been just as happy if he had been a missionary." Hugh replied, "But Mom, I *was* a missionary!"

Hugh Hefner's "missionary" work for freedom of sexual expression was very far from his mother's idea of a Christian missionary, but they listened to each other and stayed close for all those years. Listening to his mother did not mean that Hugh had to agree with her, but she always knew that he understood her perspective.

Another reason for listening to our mother is that it helps us to understand her. This may sound like a truism, but it is easily overlooked. As we develop into adolescents and then adults, we typically stop listening to our mother. We try instead to listen to ourself and to our peers; this is a natural part of the maturing process. But once we have grown up, if we persist in not listening to our mother, we may not understand her as one adult to another. In fact, we may find that we listen to our friends more closely, in order to understand their point of view and get closer to them, than we do to our mother.

In learning to listen to our mother today, it is important not to confuse her with our "inner mother," the internal image of her we developed over the years, who still talks to us as if we were children. It is easy to make the mistake of hearing what she says now through the filter of that internal image. Also, she might want to talk about issues—concerning, for instance, our relationships—but if we are usually unavailable to listen seriously to her, she might feel reluctant to broach important matters with us. Learning to manage our relationship with our mother really does require us to be able to see things from her side, to listen to her as the adult she is.

Mike Pierce related an incident with his mother that became a family joke, a story trotted out for amusement, until he realized how his mother really felt about it. "Once when I was three or four years old, she had taken me with her shopping, and she left me in the supermarket. She went all the way home before she realized I wasn't there! My older sister brought my absence to her attention, and she rushed back to the supermarket. I was in the cereal aisle and feeling no pain! It is something that the whole family has always teased her about. But I didn't realize until recently, listening to her reaction to the family telling the story, how much it really hurt her to be reminded of it, so it was kind of insensitive on our part. Now I protect her when they still try to kid her about it."

Mike's realization changed his underlying view of his mother, whom he had generally regarded as a strong person. He appreciates now that she has sensitive areas and can be hurt by jokes concerning how she "failed" as a mother.

Sometimes, even when we have a good relationship with our mother and feel that we know her, we can be taken by surprise at the strength of her reaction to events or to things we say. "When David and I decided to get married, Mother was the last one we told," Nicole Farhi said. "When I finally told her, we were out with her and my brother at an art fair in Paris. I told her I had some wonderful news: 'I'm going to get married!' She was so shocked. She asked my brother if he knew, and he said, 'Yes, I'm very pleased.' Then we met lots of my friends, and she asked if they knew and they all said, 'Yes.' She realized she was the last one to find out, and she was very upset."

In fact, the reason Nicole left her for last was positive: "I wanted it to be special for my mother. I didn't want to tell her over the phone; I wanted to wait until I could see her, when she came to us in Paris in October, and we could celebrate together." In telling David's children from his first marriage, his ex-wife, and their various friends quite carefully to avoid hurting them and to share the excitement with them, Nicole's mother got left out.

Nicole says now that what she did was "stupid," because she ought to have known it would be a mistake to leave her mother until last. She realized she had misjudged how her mother would feel about being the last one to be told. It is an understandable mistake, but one that reminds us how important it is not to take for granted that we "know" our mother, but to keep on listening to her so we understand how best to relate to her.

It helps to find issues you share in your lives that you can talk about readily. Sometimes these issues, useful as they are for helping you listen to your mother, can present themselves in an unwelcome fashion. Last year my husband had to have a hip replacement. On a Wednesday, the week before his operation, we went to visit his mother. We carefully explained to her that John would not be able to see her for about ten weeks while he was in the hospital and convalescing. On that Thursday, exactly one week before his surgery, Muriel fell from her bed and broke the same hip! However, this did not faze her; she called from her hospital bed and told her son what to expect. It then turned into a competition of how much quicker, better, and more readily she did things than him! When he rang to tell me in my office, I just laughed. She could not stand for him to have the attention, care, and concern from others that she felt she needed and should have by right! But there was a silver lining in this cloud, in that they suddenly had a lot to talk about for the first time in years.

Recently I found myself sitting on an airplane next to

Peter Gabriel, who was at one time with the rock group Genesis and is now a composer of his own work. I told him about this book, and he started to speak about his mother. He was a great admirer of John Lennon and told me how much he liked the song John had written for his mother. Although Peter had just finished a song for his father, he was finding writing a song for his mother more difficult. He loves her a lot, but finds it hard to express it directly. He recounted how an American musician, Djivan Gasparyan, had performed a song for his mother to Peter, which ended with both of them in tears. I suggested that if he tried listening to his mother now as an adult in her own right and less as his mother, he might be able to connect with her more closely and gain some inspiration for his song. It's a way of tuning in to our mother—both metaphorically and, for Peter, literally!

> Listen with an open mind to what your mother says. You can let her know that you can understand her point of view without sharing it. Really listening to her helps you understand her better. Your mother may have important things to say; she may even be very wise.

Remember That Your Mother Has a Past

Sometimes our early memories of our mother are of a woman who seemed to belong to a world of mystery and sophistication, for she was experiencing a life well beyond our childhood understanding. Mia Farrow described such a recollection of her mother, Maureen O'Sullivan. "My mother, moving gracefully through the house and garden, arranging flowers, breakfasting on a white wicker tray in her bedroom, was easily the most beautiful creature imaginable. Her voice was soft, with a light Irish accent. She seemed possessed of magical qualities and an unending supply of stories. At night I lay in bed listening for the rustle of silk or taffeta, waiting for her perfume to overpower the scent of jasmine." But it is easy for us, in growing up, to forget that our mother had a life before we grew older and just knew her as our mother.

When Greg Gorman's mother died recently, he told me, "I had a lot of regrets that I just didn't know enough about her and her life, and I'm still dealing with that at this point." A key step in managing our relationship with our mother is to find out about her early life. People who have asked their mother for this sort of background information sometimes hear revealing stories.

Josephine David's mother, now in her fifties, has recently remarried, and lives in Palm Springs, California, where she manages a large house for a wealthy couple. The story of her past made interesting listening for Josephine. "My mother came from a very wealthy family on the East Coast. She was a debutante and lived a prominent social life. But she really hated it, because she felt pressured to be "social," to go to the right schools and all that kind of thing. So she asked her parents to send her to a college in Colorado—the farthest place away she could find from her parents' home in Greenwich, Connecticut.

"At college she met my father, who was from a radically different background. He was a very poor, Catholic son of a police officer. She got pregnant as fast as she could, and she and my father got married. They settled in Colorado. Her parents gave up on my mother." Josephine's mother felt she was free at last.

This brief story says a lot about Josephine's mother, especially her past, before Josephine was born. She was driven by her disaffection with, and need to escape from, her high society upbringing, as well as her desire to assert her independence. Knowing more of her mother's past has given Josephine a sense of connection with her mother that she could not necessarily have gained from knowing about her life only after those turbulent, early years.

Some pasts are quite tragic—as was that of Mike Nichols's mother. "First she was a famous beauty in her circles in Germany," he said. "Her parents were sort of literary stars. Her mother was a poet; her father was an important writer who, at the time, was part of the Weimar government, the two-week provisional government, and when that government disintegrated, he was beaten to death by police soldiers. She was orphaned very early and brought up by a half-sister, who made her and her younger sister very, very unhappy. When she married my father, who was a Russian doctor, she began suffering from a series of illnesses. That was when we came from Germany to the United States as refugees. She had to come a year later than the rest of us because she was in the hospital. After my father died young of leukemia, she met her next husband, my stepfather, who was also a doctor and died at forty-four. She was ill most of her life, with terrible neuralgia, and then became addicted for a long time to a painkiller that was a sort of aspirin."

Nicole Farhi's mother suffered much during World War

II. "My parents are both Jewish-Turkish. They met in France, in the Jewish community, and married young, for love. They were in their twenties when the war broke out, and because they were Jews, they had to go into hiding. They hid for two years on a little farm, and my mother became pregnant with my brother. They hoped they would survive the war undiscovered, but they were denounced by someone in the village and had to escape at night. She does speak to me about the war, and I think it is important to know what she went through in her past; it is a part of her life that must have affected her deeply. I want her to tell my daughter about it, too."

Sometimes, in learning about our mother's past we can construct her story by piecing together what we learn about her upbringing and her memories, and then, into this vision, placing our own observations of our mother. If we can tell our mother's life in the form of a story, it encourages us to think about her life as her experience rather than as a mere recounting of events from the viewpoint of an external observer. This process helps us to understand her. And if we examine the story we have constructed from time to time, we can amend the details if it appears that certain elements of it no longer fit how we see things, or if we acquire new information from our mother or others.

Guiseppe Bruno owns two of the most successful Italian restaurants in New York with his three brothers. He came from Italy with his family as a teenager to settle in the United States. His sense of his mother's past as a story is unique to him and her, but probably also reflects the experiences of many immigrant families to America. It is a story of a kind of mothering that is less common now, from a culture in which a mother was expected to live for her family. In its detail and content it may be very different from the story you would construct for your mother, but it gives an idea of the areas you might cover.

"My mother comes from a good family," he began. "Her father was mayor of a small village in southern Italy. My father grew up with no father; his father died when my father was six months old. My father's family was poor, so he was forced to work twenty-four hours a day. Where we come from, life is more primitive than here. My mother and father lived next door to each other when they were children. They liked each other, and so when my mother was eighteen and my father was about twenty, they got married. They had kids right away. My mother suffered for the first ten years of her marriage because her father had not wanted her to marry my father. He had finally agreed because their village was small and she and my father were already going out, and who would marry my mother then? Nobody. But my mother's father would not speak to her for the first three or four years of her marriage.

"So the children were born one after the other—me and my three brothers are all one year apart. We had a farm, with sheep and other domestic animals to take care of. After a while my mother did not really accept my father anymore, but there was nothing she could say because a woman, where we come from, obeys. But, even though she was not at all a happy woman, she was very loyal. My father began to gamble in card games. My mother objected and the atmosphere in the house was very bad. When my father was out of the house, my mother would admonish us children never to follow his bad example.

"Although my family was Catholic, we never went to church. In the small village community this was difficult, but my mother could not force my father to go, and he would not go because if he did he would have had to go to confession and admit to his gambling. And it was not done to go to church as a wife without your husband.

"I remember my mother was always tired when I was a small boy. She used to press shirts and underwear and socks, everything, because she believed that a woman has to make men look good and that a mother can do things for her children that no one else can. She didn't like us to go to school dirty or with a torn shirt. I remember her cleaning my youngest brother and my sister. She was always cleaning and working. But despite all this work, she would entertain us at night. In the 1960s in my village there was still no electricity, so as soon as the sun went down we would sit around the fire, and she used to tell us stories about our grandfather and grandmother. Sometimes she used to tell stories that would scare us, and we would try to stay up as long as possible until we were so tired we weren't scared anymore, and then we would finally fall into bed.

"But in those years, my mother was sad, because my father was never there—he was out gambling and so on. But she was so kind and faithful to him, because she was proud. She didn't want anybody to talk badly about us. Now that I look back, I can see that a lot of women where we come from accepted that role, just because they didn't want people to talk badly about them and their children. Today things are different. Women are more free to do as they want—especially here in America.

"In the 1970s, in that part of Italy, there was the beginning of a big Mafia movement. We had a lot of strikes and the schools closed. My mother said to my father, 'We're leaving. If you want to come, sell whatever you have to sell, because we are going to America.' It was a brave and slightly crazy decision! But we came, my father too, and we got work, and my mother continued to look after us. We worked hard, and eventually my brothers and I got the restaurants.

"After all my mother has done for us, I am very grateful. Once I got a chance to show my appreciation. I bought her a beautiful red dress, and I said, 'Mama, I want to take you out tonight.' I took her and my sister to a restaurant. As we sat in there, I could see she was uncomfortable, but I didn't know why. I said, 'Mama, what's going on?' She wouldn't say, but my sister said, 'I think there is a man looking at Mom.' A man was looking at her, admiringly, and she was embarrassed. I had to laugh. My mother is beautifully dressed, I've taken her out and I want to make her feel good, and all she says is, 'Oh, this is so embarrassing!' I said, 'Do you want me to go and tell him not to look at you?' She said, 'No, are you crazy? You can't do that! Imagine how embarrassing that would be!' But I know she enjoyed the attention, really. She wasn't used to it, and for weeks she couldn't stop talking about how she went out and someone was looking at her. She was so flattered.

"Now that she is an old lady, I always say to her, 'Don't worry about me, because I want you to be at peace with yourself. I know how the world is, and how to look after myself.' I think it's the dream of every mother to see that her kids are okay, and I want my mother not to have to worry anymore, because that's been the most difficult thing about her life: She has had to worry so much."

Guiseppe's account of his mother's life is a mixture of family history, personal reminiscences, judgments about her, and anecdotes about their times together. However similar to or different from this our own mother's story is, it will almost certainly be helpful in clarifying for us the nature of her past, our understanding of her now, and our feelings about her. So try writing the story of your mother's past and bring it up to the present. It could be an important step toward improving your relationship with her.

> Remember that your mother had a life before you were born. Find out about it so you can know her better as a person. Her past had a big influence on your present. Do you know her story?

Ask Your Mother Simply and Directly How You Can Make Her Life Better

When I was fifteen, my mother was dying of cancer. I was aware that my mother was ill, but I did not realize how seriously. That year, I was determined to give her the best possible time for her birthday. For her birthday treat I bought her a gorgeous red dress, just as Guiseppe had for his mother, and announced that I was going to take her out on the town, drive up and down Main Street to see the sights, and then go to see a film. But the driving up and down made my mother feel sick, and so she finally said, "Honey, I don't think I want to go to the movies after all. But I've had just the best time coming out with you. Thank you for my birthday treat." It was her last birthday; she died the following year.

This memory is painful for me, because in trying to do

the right thing, I got it wrong: I was not able to see things from my mother's point of view. In wanting to make her life better, I did not ask her what she wanted but just did what I thought was best. I was young, but even when we grow to adulthood, many of us remain trapped in a childlike (and self-centered) conception of what our mother wants.

Bill Smullen praises his mother for her generosity. She spent a large part of her life being a caregiver: in addition to raising her children, she looked after Bill's father for twenty-four years after he suffered a stroke. He wishes now that he had asked her one question: "What could I have done to make your life better?"

Few of us openly ask our mother what she would like us to do for her, and yet I have seen people find it one of the most direct and effective ways to improve their relationship with her. Simply asking the question says so much about our intentions for our relationship with her. Of course, in doing so we do need to be prepared to try to help in the ways that she asks.

People who have asked their mother this question often find that what she really wants is more frequent communication. At the least, she wants to be called more often. While this sounds like an easy step, a moment's thought reminds us that it can be a difficult task calling her regularly.

Colin Powell's mother is now dead, but he still keeps in touch with one of his aunts. "She is my father's sister and is now ninety-three. She never married or had any children, and so she regards me essentially as her child. My father called her practically every day of his life, and when he died, I took over the responsibility. I can't call her every day, but I call every week. She's just like my mother, and the conversation is as I imagine it would be with my mother:

"'Hello Beryl, how are you?'

"'Fine, darling, fine.' I have a hard time understanding her; she's never lost her pidgin accent—not one inch improvement in the seventy-five years she's been in this country.

"'How are you feeling?'

"'Oh, I'm not so good. The shoulder hurts, the knee hurts. . .' and I listen to the details of her ailments for a while.

"'Well, we're all fine. The children are fine. Did anybody come see you?'

"'Well, yes, Claret, my cousin, was here Sunday.'"

Colin then gets the list of visitors. He finds the calls hard work, but he feels right making these weekly calls, for they are a way he can try to make Beryl's life better as she wants it.

Sometimes a pragmatic way of helping your mother is to help her to do something she would find difficult to do by herself. "My mother told me she wanted a computer," Josephine David said. "She had seen the woman she works for getting on to the Internet, and she thought it would be nice if she could send E-mails to me. I helped her look through the ads and find a computer that sounded good. I don't think she would have been confident enough to buy it if I hadn't been there to help her. It was nice to be able to do that for her. I set her up with America Online and taught her how to send E-mails. She's got the hang of it now, and she E-mails me almost every day."

Most mothers do not ask for a lot of help when asked how we can make their lives better; it is time and support for the smaller but troublesome aspects of life that they really appreciate.

Internet use is now so common that it is easy to forget that, for a generation that grew up without it, it may be a little confusing getting started. But e-mail messages are less intrusive into our time than telephone calls, and we may find this an ideal way to keep in touch with our mother, and for her to feel that she can communicate with us without becoming a nuisance.

Letters and faxes can help, too. Bill Goldman's mother was profoundly deaf, and the two of them had great difficulty conversing over the telephone. This drove Bill to distraction, until it was suggested that he fax his mother in advance with the topics of conversation he wished to discuss. It made their conversations easier; as a result, they were able to communicate better.

Mary Lou Shields had the experience, familiar to some of us, of being with her mother but wanting to be elsewhere. "When I was young, I used to find my mother great fun. But later in her life when I would go to visit her, I really would have preferred spending the evening having dinner with friends. I felt guilty about it, especially when I remember how she used to always go out of her way to do things for me during difficult times. Like when my friends were getting party dresses and she didn't have the money to buy me one, she learned how to sew and made sure that way that I had a 'designer' dress."

Feeling guilty about not enjoying time with our mother can be uncomfortable, but it stems largely from assuming that we should find such occasions as much fun as being with our friends. In fact, the important thing is that we are doing something for our mother, and should feel pleased that we are able to do that, rather than feeling obliged to also enjoy it. But if it becomes hard work, as it did for Mary Lou, thinking back to the things she did for us to make our life better can help to motivate us.

While it is often the smaller details of life with which our mother would like help, there are times when it is clear that she needs much greater help, which might require us to interrupt our own life in a big way. When Philipe France moved from Paris to live in the United States, he left his mother behind. Then she was diagnosed with cancer. He asked her how he could make her life better, and what she really wanted was to spend time with him. So Philipe arranged for her to come to the United States. "I took a leave of absence from my work, bought a huge truck and trailer, and we went all around the States for three months."

Hearing about gestures like this, when someone's mother needs urgent and substantial help, is encouraging for those of us whose mother is asking from us smaller ways of making her life better; it keeps in proper perspective our small sacrifices of time and effort. And in considering the ways we may be able to help, it is important to remember that our overall aim is to improve our relationship with our mother. That is good for them, and good for us.

One of the most challenging times for us in helping our mother's quality of life is when she faces death. Greg Gorman was with his mother every day during the last two weeks of her life. "It was very hard. She had suffered from chronic emphysema, and she'd been in and out of the hospital over the last few years. But within two days of her last admission to the hospital they wanted to put her in intensive care so they could watch her more closely. I was in favor of that, because I thought it would give her a chance for more medical attention if she was having trouble. But when I went to the hospital on Wednesday morn-ing they had her on a ventilator. She was mostly unconscious, and she never really came back during that two weeks, which was really rottten. On several occasions she would open her eyes a couple of times, and she'd be able to answer questions for me just by a nod or look. But it was very rough on my brothers and myself—very, very difficult. The doctors just wanted to do the surgery. She was a very frail eighty-three-year-old woman at that point, and her health was shot. She never wanted to be on a life support system. It took me about a week before I could talk to the doctors and let them know that I didn't want them to do the surgery. I wanted her life support system turned off." Greg had a disagreement with one of his brothers. "My mother was his whole life and his only great true friend. She took care of him and he took care of her. The last thing he wanted to do was pull the plug."

But Greg and his other brother prevailed, and they saved their mother from the operation. "Both my brothers and my younger brother's wife, we were all with her when she passed away. We'd go home and shower and sleep for maybe 5 or 6 hours, but otherwise we were at the hospital around the clock." Greg worked hard at helping his mother, but even so he has regrets that he did not do more earlier. "I realized about six months before that I needed to start spending more time with my mother. It really pisses me off now that I knew in the back of my mind that there wasn't that much time left, and I really, deeply regret that I did not spend more time with her, even though I took care of her and I loved her very much. I was a good son and I think she would be the first person to tell you that. But it still affects me deeply when I think about it now."

Reflecting on his experience leads him to encourage others to do all they can, when they can, while it is still possible. "The only thing I can say is for those people who still have their mother, whether they have a good relationship or a bad relationship, I really advise them to get through those parts and get to know their parents and spend as much time with them as possible."

> Ask your mother how you can make her life better. Often all she wants is to communicate more regularly. Or you could help her practically, with something she might have trouble doing. Help her maintain her quality of life for as long as you can.

Ask Your Mother About Your Childhood History

My family died when I was young. When I was undergoing my psychoanalytic training, my tutor pointed out to me, "The sadness for you is that everyone has died, and you aren't able to ask the questions that could help to place the pieces of your life into a completed picture." And during the many years that I have practiced psychotherapy, I have often heard patients say, "Why didn't I ask my mother while she was alive? Now I will never know."

If you are fortunate enough to have living family, think of your life as a jigsaw puzzle and ask as many questions as you can to put the picture together. Throughout this book you have been encouraged to recall your life experiences with your mother and reexamine them. Part of this process involves placing your life in a historical context. Understanding your roots can help you know more clearly who you are, as part of a family—which you share with your mother—going back several generations.

My husband and I made a "roots" journey to Arizona, so that he could meet my ninety-six-year-old Aunt Flossie before she died. Talking to her, we puzzled over why six children in the family had produced only two grandchildren—a question I had never before thought to ask. She said, "Oh, that's easy— my father, who was born in the 1800s, was an only child. I always thought there was probably some inherited problem." I had always assumed that my aunts and uncles had chosen not to bear children—it had never entered my mind that there could be a genetic factor. This is something I would never have known if we had not asked, but as soon as I heard it, I felt a sense of knowing more about my family, and hence about my mother and myself. Sometimes the sort of information you get about your childhood history is not so much facts as atmosphere: a clearer understanding of the family circumstances in which you grew up. It can be especially useful to get other people who knew you in your childhood to tell you about their impressions and memories, because in this way you can see a different side to your past with your mother.

I was born eighteen years after my sister, when my parents were in their forties. In Oklahoma and other southern states of America, they called a late baby like me a "top crop." My "other mother," Henrietta, our black "mammy," explained what this meant. Every year in Oklahoma, the cotton-picking season occurred in the early autumn. School started in August, earlier than other schools in the United States, and, come October, school was let out so that everyone in the community could pick the top crop. It was like a big festival as the long burlap sacks were pulled down the rows of cotton. The colored workers (which is what African-Americans were called when I was little) singing wonderful songs, the hot dirt between our toes, and the drone of the bees—it's one of my fondest memories. Henrietta explained to me that children who are born to older parents in her culture were called top crops because they brought such joy in later life.

I knew that my late arrival was something of an embarrassment for my parents. But hearing the other side of the story from Henrietta gave me a more positive feeling about the fact of my birth late in my parents' lives.

Sometimes finding missing pieces of our life's jigsaw can be more dramatic. Once I was somewhere in the English Midlands in a car with a driver. We started chatting, and he told me that he had been placed at birth with a foster family. He had a more or less idyllic childhood. When he reached adulthood his foster parents asked him if he would like to know a bit more about his infancy. They had very few details: the village he was from and the house his mother had lived in at the time she gave the baby away.

He decided to take a sentimental journey back to this village. On arriving at the doorstep of the house that was once his mother's home, a neighbor, seeing a stranger, asked if she could help. When he told her who he was looking for, the neighbor helpfully explained that she had married and moved to a nearby village, and gave him his mother's married name. He found her number through Information and sure enough, his mother and her husband still lived there. So he went to see her, as a surprise. His mother was quite shocked but nevertheless pleased to see him.

Now comes the twist. This man had an identical twin brother whom his mother had kept. "I was curious," he said. "Why did she keep him and not me?" She had no answer, saying only that she could not afford to keep both babies. He said he did not feel upset about it. "If you knew my adoptive parents, you'd understand I've been so lucky." He went to see his twin brother. "We looked very alike, and we get along great." It had been a long wait to find him, but the driver thought that fitting this large element of his life into the overall pattern of it had been very rewarding. Not everyone is so fortunate, of course. Seeking your mother in this way can be frustrating and, if you find her, even disillusioning. But many people say that they feel compelled to try, despite the emotional risks.

A childhood friend called me recently. When we were small, she used to visit our house often. She had recently been undergoing psychotherapy, and she explained that she had been telling her analyst that my mother was constantly in her memories, almost like a part of herself.

She had said to her analyst, "We were very wealthy, but when I went to Alyce Faye's house, which was very poor, it was always calm and nice. Her mother had a painting of Jesus Christ knocking at the door to get in, with the words 'Knock and ye shall enter,' from the Bible. Visiting Alyce Faye's home I felt I had been let inside, just as He was. There was a den with everything to expand the mind: puzzles, books, paints, things to do.

"When we were very little we would lie in Alyce Faye's bed, and there were two things I remember. One was a beautiful poem her grandmother had embroidered on silk:

Now I lay me down to sleep,
I pray the Lord my soul to keep,
If I should die before I wake,
I pray the Lord my soul to take.

"The second item," my friend continued to her analyst, "was glow-in-the-dark stars her mother had put on the ceiling to represent the night sky. Alyce Faye's mother gave me something that I have carried with me the rest of my life." This call impressed upon me how some of the details of my childhood home that my mother created are still so much a part of my life. The poem embroidered on silk had been important only recently, when my first granddaughter, Phoebe, was stillborn: I gave this very same poem, the original one embroidered in silk, to my son and daughter-in-law. And just before I had received this call from my friend, I had bought similar glow-in-the-dark stars for my second granddaughter, just as my mother had for me.

Our childhood homes can nourish us and help us to establish roots for our life, a deep and stable base from which we can grow and branch into areas and activities far and wide. Facts about the nature of that home are pieces of the puzzle, too. For most of us, it was our mother who created its aura and atmosphere. So ask your mother, or those who knew her, to tell you the facts about your life.

Ask your mother about your own childhood. It can give you a better understanding of the family circumstances in which you grew up. Your life is like a jigsaw puzzle. Ask your mother to help you find the missing pieces.

Get to Know Your Mother's Extended Family

After Greg Gorman's mother died, he came across some family photographs. "The first weekend after she had passed away, I brought a few of her things over to my house, including a box of family pictures. I went through that box in one night, mostly pictures I hadn't seen in family albums. I found pictures of tons of people I didn't know—and it was very special seeing extraordinary pictures of her in her early life, a life that I hadn't known. I hadn't spent the time to look through them with her, to hear the extenuating circumstances that had brought about the moment when the pictures were taken.' He wishes now he had known more about all the people in the photographs with his mother, for "I would have liked to have known a lot about her upbringing and her life as a young adult." Memories directly involving our mother also put us back in touch in our mind with relations, friends, and other people who were associated with our mother and were in a way part of her. It can be surprising how rich these recollections can be in giving us an insight into the emotional world of our upbringing. They provide a perspective on our mother which, while tangential, gives her a dimension which sometimes helps us to understand her better than if we concentrate only on memories directly involving her.

In recalling his early years with his mother, Colin Powell had such an experience, for he found that some of the influences his mother had on him were because of her like-minded friends and relatives. Hearing his story gives an idea of some of the recall that can easily happen once you start thinking about your mother's family.

"There was always a lot of laughter in the house," he said. "There was always fun. The human condition was a source of comedy." This atmosphere of enjoyment came from some of the other people present as well as his mother. "We had an assortment of characters in the family," he went on. "Not only cousins and aunts and uncles—we had plenty of those—but also strange characters who were always passing through our house in Harlem, people such as Mackintosh the Mover and Vincent the Painter. These are stories I haven't thought of in years—never told anybody."

The return of these people into his conscious mind after a long absence made him realize how much they were part of the atmosphere. "Mackintosh—I don't know if that was his first name or his last—was a Jamaican, who you went to when you had to move from one tenement to another. He would come with his barrels—in those days you didn't have those fancy boxes, you had big barrels—and start to pack one barrel, and then say, 'God, I'm tired. It's time for a drink.' Then Macintosh and his movers would all start drinking, and before you knew it, it might take a week to get a one-day move in between all the partying and the drinking. I just thought it was wonderful and charming. Vincent the Painter was another Jamaican, and whenever we needed our little forty-dollar-a-month apartment painted, he would do it. The fact was these tenements had walls that weren't worth painting, but you had to have yours painted every two years or else you weren't keeping up. It was a matter of prestige to have Vincent the Painter paint your wall. But one never knew when he would show up. He would say he would be there on Monday and would show up on Thursday. He would examine paint sploshes on the walls as if he was Van Gogh and, when he checked the ceiling, you'd have thought you'd hired Michelangelo to do the Sistine Chapel. Finally he'd get around to it, having a drink at every opportunity. It might take a month to get a room painted, but it had been done by Vincent the Painter!"

The characters Colin was recalling felt to him like an extended family of "uncles and aunts," as he called them, but they were seldom related by blood. They and his parents had emigrated to New York together and stayed in close contact all their lives. "The big thing was Sundays and holidays," Colin said. "On Sundays we would always get in the car and drive to those relatives who had gone upscale. The big thing that counted in my family, and which remains so indelibly printed on my memory, are the family parties on holidays and anniversaries. The same folk would be invited, this extended group of 'uncles' and 'aunts,' cousins and noncousins. Food would be abundant, and a lot of rum would flow. There was usually a band of some kind, a little thrown-together band, and a lot of dancing. It was a time to gather together, and to tell stories. And lies! And it was a time to misbehave slightly, to get overdrunk. For a youngster growing up in such a family, these were a remarkable set of characters. I got my sense of humor from my mother, but all these other people were a part of her world."

Another character came to his mind. "And then there was Bookie the Seaman. He used to be a bookie, but he later became an officer in the merchant marines. His real name was Cyril Davies—it took us years to find out his real name. He was a very white-skinned type, much whiter than me, with a gravelly voice and powerful build. He went away to sea for his whole life, working for the Esso company on tankers, and he would surface about once a year. And when Bookie surfaced it was a time of great rejoicing and fun, because the first thing he did when he landed was buy a Cadillac. He always bought a new one. He had all this money saved up from his latest tour of duty and, with no family, all he had was his money. He'd come around to the house in his new Cadillac—'Bookie's here, let's go cruising'—and he'd take my family. We would just drive round Harlem and show off, spending money. The kids could always expect Bookie to pull out his stack of money at some point and peel off ten, twenty, a hundred dollars and give it to you, which was a fortune. Bookie was always good for a touch. It was just a joy when Bookie or any of these others characters drifted in— Vincent the Painter or Mackintosh the Mover. What they left is tradition and roots, and I think that people miss so much in life when they don't have this extended kinship. I try to be kind to people. I learned that from her and her extended family. A warmth about life. A little conservatism in what I do. And a sense of humor."

Colin was describing here a kind of emotional memory that places his mother in a broader context, as part of something larger; a memory that is made up of deep psychological rhythms connecting us to her in a way that is best communicated in remembered stories and characters. He thinks of remembering his mother in context as an archetypal process, which is reflected across the natural world, in which consciousness of other animals seems to take on the form of a kind of tribal memory.

"I watch nature shows," he explained, "and see how an

elephant mother takes care of and teaches the baby elephant, and then how they seem to be aware of death and the passing of generations. When they come across a skeleton of a dead elephant, they touch and smell it, and look at it, and seem to be trying to remember. We don't know quite what they're doing, but we can see that the baby elephants are watching, and something is being passed on by this behavior."

Colin sees this animal behavior as a metaphor for understanding the archetypal significance of the passing on of familial warmth, rituals, memories, and love across human generations. It provides a context for his understanding of his mother, and what he learned from her, by appreciating the extended human family in which she lived when he was young.

> Find a link to your mother through her chain of friends and her extended family. They can provide a perspective on your mother that can help you understand her better.

Decide What Personality Traits You Share with Your Mother

At some point in our youth, we have all said to ourselves, "I would never do that," determining not to repeat the mistakes of our mothers. Yet despite such resolutions, as adults—and even more so as parents—we often find ourselves repeating the patterns that were imprinted so deeply during the years of our childhood.

"You know, George Bernard Shaw said, 'It's better for a parent to be a horrible warning than a good example,'"

Michael Winner, producer of the *Death Wish* films, said mischievously. "I certainly have personality traits of my mother. She would enter a restaurant, say, or a hairdresser, as an unbelievably charming and adorable woman. However, the second something happened she didn't like, she would turn into the most cutting, dreadful person. I do that, and I say to myself, 'Stop it, you are getting like your mother.'"

Most of us have mixed feelings about taking after our mother. We might feel fine about it if we are considering her more laudable qualities. But often we feel compelled to reject the idea that we share those personality characteristics we do not admire. Of course, we often do take after her, either because we have inherited some predisposition biologically—in which case we feel really stuck—or because our mother's shaping of us in childhood and our years of observing her as a role model have led to our becoming very like her. We need to reach an understanding of what our mother's characteristics are, to give ourselves a sense of which ones we have inherited and a balanced view of how we feel about them.

It can be tough when people expect us to take after our mother. "People would pat me on the head as a child and say, 'Are you going to grow up and be another little Maggie?'" said Karen Stewart. If the effect of such expectation sinks deep enough, we may even feel that we ought to follow in her footsteps. "For years I had a terrible guilt about not doing law like her. I decided that I really did not want to do that, but, even so, I'm middle-aged now and, as recently as eight years ago, I was still agonizing over whether I should have been a lawyer!"

Most of us find that there are things our mother did that are definitely not for us, and we have to face up to this and follow our own path. Trying to be like our mother because other people want us to be that way can be a recipe for frustration and anger later. Our feelings of guilt at following our own path are a natural reaction to this social pressure and do not necessarily indicate that we are making a mistake.

However, I have found in my work with adolescents that they often disparage their mother's qualities just because they belong to their mother, and they want to be as different as possible in developing their own identity. This tendency afflicts us all from time to time. And yet it can be rewarding to accept specific qualities we feel we have acquired from our mothers: "Like my mother, I have a precise mind," Karen said. "If I want to find something out, it never escapes me. Run something by me and, if it doesn't fit, six months later I'll come back to it and find where that piece fits." We can enjoy these good qualities without having to emulate our mother's choices.

Of course, we may find it uncomfortable that all this sifting and considering involves acknowledging that there are characteristics of our mother—and, perhaps, ourself—that we simply dislike. However, taking after our mother does lift a little of the responsibility from our shoulders for those aspects of our personality that are not so admirable! "I don't think she has ever been an easy woman," Karen admitted. "I don't think any members of that side of the family are too easy, and I have certainly inherited some of their characteristics. I am short-tempered, and, when my partner occasionally does the wrong thing, I bark." However, she finds it easier to accept her short temper by believing that she inherited it from her mother. Accepting what we have inherited is an important part of accepting ourselves for who we are. And recognizing the less attractive qualities we share with her keeps us close to our mothers, like partners in crime.

Nancy Blackmore shares her mother's impatience. "There was no warning. She would react with a flash of anger when something wasn't going right," she said. "I have realized that I have the same trait. I will start slamming cabinet doors, or doing something like that, when I am really ticked off. I think I hold on to my anger longer than she does, though." But Nancy recognizes that her mother has a wide range of talents to counterbalance her impatience, some of which she shares, too. "She does a lot of things. She paints, she is a photographer, she makes jewelry and sculptures. She is incredibly creative. She also writes, was an actress and has a beautiful singing voice. And I have a lot of her talents: I can sing, write, and cook. I have a decent eye as a photographer, although not the visual sense she has."

So Nancy has made a balanced audit of her inherited characteristics, both the genetic ones of nature and the learned ones of nurture. This is the sort of mature reflection which helps us to establish a stable understanding of ourselves, our mothers, and our relationships with them. Of course, even when we are aware of our mother's positive qualities, we sometimes we find ourselves repeating our mother's mistakes—for example, in our personal relationships.

"In my relationship with Roger, I repeated a lot of what my mother did in her relationship with my father," said Pamela Bridlington. "It was an appeasing relationship: he had to be pleased at all costs. My mother would say, 'You must look after him, he mustn't be allowed to get cross, we've all failed if he has one of his outbursts, he's the head of the house,' and so on."

She remembered a specific parallel between her mother's attitude and her own: "My father was jealous of my handicapped brother and resentful of the attention my mother gave him. My father would go very quiet, not saying what he was thinking, and then have an outburst. That's exactly what Roger would do. And in fact I think my assumption was, like my mother, that women were like a ball and chain to men, that they were weak and that men had a nice time without them. And so Roger and I did not marry because I felt being a wife was being the equivalent to a boring nuisance, and I did not want to tie him down."

Carol Crow described how she takes after her mother in the details of domestic homemaking. "Somebody was saying to me about my new house, 'Does it feel like your house yet?' and I said, 'Yes, it does, but oddly enough, it also feels like my mother's house.' I think I planned a lot of it to be like her house—where I keep things, how I have the kitchen and bathroom. My house reminds me of her house, and I like that."

What was it that had encouraged Carol to set up her home in ways that echoed her mother? Was it particular qualities of her childhood home that she wished to emulate or was it a more general way of keeping her mother's presence with her? Or perhaps she is similar to her mother in character, and therefore naturally created a similar home environment? There are some more superficial resemblances between them. "I have a lot of her mannerisms. And I have those odd moments when I glance at my reflection and get a shock because I look like my mother. I will say, 'There is me . . . Oh no, it's my mother!'" But when it comes to deeper aspects of personality, she feels the similarity ends. She feels that her mother has more inner strength than she does. "I haven't gone through the hardships that she has, and I thank God that I haven't been tested in that way. Perhaps I have different strengths, like self-confidence." In identifying characteristics you share, it seems that you may be similar in some ways, even emulating aspects of your mother's domestic life, while being deeply different in other areas of your makeup.

Sometimes the personality traits we share with our mother are less obvious because they are not expressed in the same way. In 1991, Douglas Coupland's first novel, *Generation X,* earned him a reputation as the voice of a generation, and he has gone on to publish other very successful books. He is close to his mother and says, "We talk, talk, talk ever since I can remember." At school, Coupland was doing well studying science, but eventually realized that he hated it. She supported him in making the big decision to give it up and go to art school instead. When he left school, his father wanted Douglas to be a doctor. The economy was in recession, and earning a living was difficult, but Douglas decided against the security of a medical career. "Even though I was scraping trying to make a living, I decided to write fiction," he says. "I was cheered on by my mom." Still today she encourages him in many things he does, even when he is not with her. "Whenever I have a scheme she gives me the gift of just not getting stuck. She lives inside of me, saying, 'Oh, just do it!'"

Douglas feels that one reason she understands him so well is that she also has a strong creative side. He recently went with her to Manitoba to see where she lived when she was growing up. Seeing scenes of her young life reinforced for him his belief that "She could have been anything. She sells herself short and says she couldn't write a Post-it note, whereas she says to me that I'm so creative. But she is creative, and I would pay anything to help her live up to her potential."

Even if your mother has not expressed her talents and traits in the way you have, if you look deeper you may see shared characteristics that will help you feel close to her.

Terry Jones thinks that the most obvious way he shares his mother's traits is physically: "I look so much like my mum!" he said. "Especially when I dress up as a woman!" And it is true—as an actor in his Monty Python drag persona, Terry does look just like his mother! So men, too, can share their mother's appearance. But a more subtle way in which men take after their mother is by choosing life partners who are like their mothers. A mother can be such a powerful force in a son's life that it is almost inevitable she will be in the minds of many men, consciously or unconsciously, positively or negatively, when they are forming relationships with women. The more we are aware of this, the better able we are to avoid replaying themes in our lives through habit rather than choice. "With my first partner I think I was very much recapitulating the father-daughter relationship my father had with my mother," said Eric Potter. "But it was partly conscious. I liked being the strong one in charge and feeling I was helping my wife to cope. In my second marriage, I have repeated the pattern. I thought I was getting into something that was a marriage of equals but, at an unconscious level, I had again chosen someone who needed me to look after her and who saw me as someone upon whom she could rely."

John Cleese has noticed several similarities between his wife and his mother. "My mother tends to chatter, and to talk in an almost bewildering sequence of 'cuts,' by which you retrace every family tree in town, cutting from one family to the next without pause for breath. You find yourself being told that the man who used to live in that house, there, who was married to the woman who used to be the housekeeper for Mr. So-and-So, whose father used to be the butcher before he married the daughter of the optician on the corner of the High Street ... and I find my wife very like that, too. The chapter in my autobiography on my relationship with my wife is going to be entitled 'In Search of a Sequitur.' So this kind of scattered chatter is characteristic of both my wife and my mother.

"Also, Alyce Faye finds it quite difficult to be still. 'Blue-arsed fly disease,' we call it. She is always on the go—in a constructive way, always doing useful things—but busy, busy, busy. I think that, deep down, she doesn't feel very comfortable with being still. I think she is very like my mother in that way."

Identifying which traits we share with our mother gives us a clearer perspective on what she is like, how we came to be the way we are, and what our strengths and weaknesses might be. And by helping us to understand our mother in terms of our own characteristics, it also draws us closer to her.

> Decide which personality traits you share with your mother.
> You might find there are things you don't like. Face up to it and follow your own path. By seeing what you have in common, good and bad, it can draw you closer to her.

If You Find Your Mother Difficult, Confront the Issues That Divide You

Many of us want to have a thriving, loving relationship with our mother but find it difficult to do so. We may, for instance, have too many distressing memories of our childhood with her, or resent things she did to us or did not do for us; it can be hard for us to forgive and forget. Even if that is not the case, we may find her difficult to get along with for other reasons.

Sometimes, it is not even that there are specific problems, it is just that life with our mother can be hard work. Mickey Cornell said of his mother, "She is something, a force of nature. She is quite nice in small doses, but she doesn't come in small doses. She is on the short side, but one doesn't think of her as short because there is so much energy there. She vibrates the earth! She is a very difficult person." His father understands. "When my dad went in for a cancer operation about fifteen years ago, before he went in I sat with him, holding his hand, and he gave me and my sister things to sign. Going down the hallway, he looked up at me, and I think he thought it was probably the last time he'd see me, as he said, 'If anything happens to me I want you to take care of your mother.' I said, 'No way! You come back from that surgery! You come back, d'you hear? I am not doing it—forget it!' I was yelling at him all the way to the elevator, and he was laughing all the way."

Sometimes we *expect* to have difficulties with our mother, because we are afraid she will behave with us as she did when we were younger. And yet our mother may surprise us, if we give her the chance. When author Wally Lamb was at school, his mother had high academic expectations of him. But when he began to achieve well, she would shake her head and say, "Don't be too smart." She told him the cautionary tale of how crabs, when placed in a bucket, will try to climb to the top, but the other crabs always pull them back down. Years later, he wanted to show her his first novel. He was anxious about how she would respond to it, both because it was giving him a high profile publicly and because some of the content was rather graphic and unpleasant. His parents did not read books—they read magazines like *Ladies' Home Journal* and *Reader's Digest*. Eventually, on one of his regular Sunday visits, he left the novel for them to read. The following Sunday they did not mention it. The same thing happened the Sunday after, and Wally began to feel rather desperate. He imagined that all sorts of dire reactions and disapprovals were brewing. Finally, at the end of the month, his mother and father said they had read it and enjoyed it. When he asked why they had not said anything sooner, it turned out that it had taken them all those weeks just to read it!

But sometimes, confronting our mother with problems is unavoidable. We need to recognize when that time has come and not leave it until too late, when the rift between us has grown too large to close. Many of us find this hard to do, feeling like Jennifer Pade, who said, "I don't criticize my mother. I try to be gentle and kind to her because she has been so kind to me. I know how she feels and her fears and her worries, and that makes me very compassionate toward her." This is natural and not a bad thing, unless it means you are repressing and avoiding issues that would be better talked out between you.

If you do decide to confront your mother about difficulties in your relationship, it is usually best to do so either in person or by letter. Telephone is often not a good medium, for it is too easy for either side to terminate the conversation.

Camilla Barker has had many conflicts with her mother, who was also somewhat emotionally unstable. One of the consequences was that, when Camilla had children, she felt unable to ignore the problems with her mother and decided not to allow her mother to spend time with the children alone. This necessitated a confrontation of a kind, a clear signal that the problems between them were so deep that a clear boundary had to be drawn. So Camilla wrote a letter to her mother, explaining how she felt, and the action she proposed to take with the children. She was surprised that in confronting her mother in this way, she provoked a constructive response.

Her mother wrote back, saying: "I got your letter. I know you don't want to talk to me, and I understand why. And I understand, and completely agree, that not allowing me to be with the children is what you need in order to maintain a harmonious home for you and the family. But what I would really, really love to be, and I know I could be, is a good grandmother. I love your children."

This letter enabled Camilla and her mother to communicate positively. Camilla rose to the occasion. "I said, 'Okay.' So my father, who is divorced from my mother, agreed to go along with the children to my mother's home, plus an ex-babysitter, who's great and knows the kids well and is very familiar with the situation between me and my mother. She makes sure the kids are okay with her, and she vouched for my mother, telling me, 'Your mother is fantastic with them, even though she is unquestionably unstable.'"

If you decide to confront your mother with issues that divide you, explain to her what you find difficult in your relationship and then propose some new arrangements that you think would establish a healthier balance between you. Sometimes we hold back from establishing such boundaries because we are afraid that doing so implies we are rejecting our mother. We need to remember that being independent from our mother does not necessarily mean that we no longer love her. It means that we are allowing our mother the right to be herself and saying clearly where we need to be separate from her in order to allow ourselves to have our own freedom.

If the conflict is extreme and you cannot find a way to resolve it, you might decide to give up your relationship with your mother for a while. Some of my patients have successfully tried "trial separations," in which they had no contact with their mother for a period of time. The break from each other allowed things to simmer down, and afterward they were able to reconcile their differences and reestablish a relationship. This approach does not always work, but, since the outcome of confrontation can be a successful resolution of difficulties, it is a step well worth attempting.

Confront the issues that divide you. Explain the problem as you see it, and then propose a solution. Do this in person or by letter, never over the phone.

Take a break from your mother. It might help to sort things out.

Keep a Sense of Humor About Your Mother

When she was growing up, Penny de Jong had a difficult time with her mother. But amid the painful memories are a few incidents when the clouds dispersed and she was able to laugh. "One incident that affected me greatly, a fabulous flash in my memory, was when my twin sister and I were about eight and my older sister ten. We all had serious trouble with Mom; it was the one thing that united us. My mother had gone out for the evening and the baby-sitter was asleep. My sisters came into my room and sat on the edge of my bed, and pretty soon we started to make fun of my mother. We imitated her, getting into incredibly funny mimicries and reenactions of incidents with her. We howled with laughter—we just had a ball. It was wonderful! We had a crazy mother, and we could share that and laugh about it."

The humor that unites children who find their mother difficult can also be a source of relief for adults. Painful and frustrating though our relationship with our mother can be, realizing that we are all in the same boat is both supportive and healing. And when we hear about someone else's misfortunes with his or her mother and are amused by them, our laughter is one of recognition.

For many years, the tragedy of Alzheimer's disease was not understood, and we were appalled or amused by the inability of our aging parents to keep things straight. Of course, in its advanced stages, when sufferers cannot even recognize their own children, there is never a funny side to it. But now that we understand better the difficulties posed by Alzheimer's, we can have more empathy for both the sufferers and their families. It can result in disturbing or even very upsetting behaviors, but it helps people to cope with their forgetful parents if we also acknowledge the humor it brings—especially when our parents can laugh with us.

John Lahr's mother was very old and suffering from Alzheimer's. John was hoping that if she saw some old friends, she might regain some contact with the social world. John's mother had been a Ziegfeld girl in New York City. These beautiful and talented young women had been from several ethnic groups, and in the thirties it had been unusual to mix people like this in any form of employment. One of John's mother's fellow Ziegfeld girls had been a black woman with whom she had remained friends all of her life. So John rang the now elderly woman and asked if she would go with him to the hospital to visit his mother. As they entered the hospital room, his mother stared at the woman intently, and John felt very hopeful that she had recognized her old and dear friend. To help his mother's memory, he suggested that the friend might sing or dance something that the two girls had performed in their youth. So the older woman began to sing and do a little dance, right there in the hospital room. John's mother looked at him and then looked at the other woman. She raised her hand, pointed, and said, "Is that woman a Negro?" John and his mother's old friend just laughed. What else could they do?

Sometimes what sounds like a difficult situation when we hear about someone else's troubles with a mother has in fact been dealt with by the person with a dash of reality and a sense of humor. Recently I was traveling and met a lovely and sexy young woman whom all the boys adored. In our conversation one of the young men asked her where she was from. She said Mendocino, California. He looked surprised and laughed uncomfortably. "But that is where all the lesbians are from."

"That's right," she said. "My mom is a lesbian and she became one when I was fourteen." I could not resist saying, "But wasn't that traumatic for you, being in puberty and beginning to come to terms with your sexuality?"

She laughed and said, "Well, you would think so. But my four best friends already had lesbian moms, so I had been feeling really odd and left out. So when my mom came out it was a relief to me, because then I was like everyone else in my crowd."

Sometimes we have to keep a sense of humor about our mother's criticisms of us, and this is easier if we generally have a good relationship with her. Greg Gorman was close to his mother, and they had a loving relationship. This made it easier for him to tolerate her outspoken criticisms. When his parents divorced, he moved her out to California to be close to him: "I bought her a new car because her old car was kind of rundown. She was used to driving Cadillacs and Lincolns provided by my dad, and I bought her a Chrysler. She said, 'Really darling, but it wouldn't pull a whore out of bed on Saturdays.'"

Another time, Greg, who is a professional photographer, had just finished building a new studio in Los Angeles. He furnished it with large, heavy pieces in Tuscan and Moroccan style and proudly showed it off to his mother. She said nothing but when she brought her sister to see it, her sister asked, "What do you think of the place and Greg's furnishings?"

"Well, I think the place is beautiful," said Greg's mom.

"So what did you think of the furniture?" persisted the sister.

"I think it would make great firewood," replied Greg's mother.

Greg loves to laugh at these stories of his mother. He told me that when she died, "and we were getting ready to have the service in the Episcopalian church, I asked how long the service would last, and they said about one and a half hours. I said 'No way! My mother will get up and walk out!'"

It may even be appropriate to use humor to help our mother to deal with her problems. John Cleese discovered that this worked surprisingly well for him. "Probably the main way we communicate is through humor: she sometimes makes me laugh, and I can make her laugh. For example, I have heard the same depressed story so many times over the years—you know, 'I don't know how I can go on, I have just lived too long, what can I do about it, I don't want to be alive anymore. . .' Some days my usual empathizing doesn't help much, and once, quite spontaneously, I told her that I knew a little man in Fulham who would come down to Weston and kill her when she really did not want to live anymore. When she had had enough all she had to do was give me a call, and I would arrange it. She stared at me for about fifteen seconds and then burst out laughing. I noticed that the joke completely changed her mood, and so I started to use it regularly. 'Oh dear,' I'd say, 'is it time to call the little man in Fulham, then?' Once, when she went on about how unhappy her sister Marjorie was, I said, 'Well, he's offered me a deal: He'll do two for the price of one.' Lately I told her that the little man in Fulham had died, so she was going to have to do it herself. I showed her the window and said to her, 'Look, when you have had enough, you can just put this stool here, and jump out of the window. It'll be as easy as anything.' And she joined in, saying, 'Well, not for a couple of weeks, you know, because the weather's nice. . .' Probably when I started, I was doing it out of a kind of desperation, saying something to try to shift the mood. But it works so well. The humor gives her a capacity to stand back, so I use it."

Sinbad, the stand-up comedian, is a friend of mine. He had this to say on the topic: "Mothers. I was just with mine the other day. The thing about mothers—everyone has one, whether you're a Vietnam veteran, a criminal, a rapper. Doesn't matter. You get in trouble, and your mama's there! You know someone like Charles Manson. His father would probably say, 'Now son, I taught you better.' His mother, she would say, 'Now I know Charles killed all those people, but he's a good boy. He didn't really mean to do that, and I'm sure he wouldn't do it again.' God put mothers on earth as guardian angels. Even when you want to get away from that voice in your head, you can't. That voice keeps you on the right path."

In my psychotherapy practice I have often listened to painful stories of difficult mothers, and my patients tell me that amid all the analysis, the ideas, the techniques, and strategies for dealing with the issues, the one piece of advice I have offered them that they find most helpful is, 'Don't have a sense of humor failure about your mother.'

> Keep your sense of humor. It's okay to laugh about the things you don't like in your mother, with friends who are in the same boat. Laughter is the closest thing to tears—and can be a great healer.

Remember That Managing Your Mother Is Really About Managing Yourself

The central message of this book is that underlying any approach to "managing our mother" is the issue of how we manage ourselves. Being aware of our own emotional states, especially the impact they have on our relationship with our mother, is perhaps the most important step of all, because it makes all the others possible.

Sometimes managing ourselves in this way amounts to simply being aware of the effect on our mother of the way we are behaving emotionally. For example, one of the most common problems people experience with their mothers is that they seem not to be able to treat their children as adults and persist in behaving toward them as she did when they were young. I had an American friend who was a schoolteacher in England. Each summer she took her own children back to the States, where they all stayed with her parents. Every year when she returned to England, she would complain about how all summer her mother had treated her like a child. Finally I asked her who was responsible for doing the household chores when she was visiting her mother. Her quick answer was, "She is, of course! I'm exhausted after a year of teaching and two active children."

My friend was allowing herself to return to a childlike role of having her mother look after her. While this is understandable for a short while, we need to remember that being with our mother triggers all sorts of habits, set reactions, and assumptions that have been formed over the years, both for us and our mother. If we allow ourselves to fall into childhood patterns when we return to our mother's home, it is not surprising that they treat us like children. Behaving as adults with our mother is necessary so that she can feel more easily able to treat us as adults.

Sometimes the way we manage our emotions lies deeper in our psyche. Although Marjorie McPherson feels quite negative about her mother, she is still working on and trying to achieve a better relationship with her. "She's seventy-nine and finds it very difficult to talk about her emotions. When I'm with her, I find I change completely from my normal self. I get irritable and depressed. Recently I went to her house with my brother and my daughter for the weekend to help clear out her loft, and so I slept there for a night, which was something that I hadn't done for years. I was in floods of tears by the morning. I got into bed with Sarah, my daughter, and I said, 'I don't know what's come over me. I feel helpless. I feel full of anxiety and fear, rage and anger—you know, all these things.'

"Anxiety is an accurate word for me in describing an undercurrent that is there all the time with my mother."

The importance of Marjorie's own emotional state in determining how she gets along with her mother is confirmed by the fact that her mother gets along well with Marjorie's children. "It's a joke among my children how really het up I get when I'm going to see my mother. My daughters get on much better with her than I do because they don't have this emotional entanglement that I don't seem able to get myself free of."

Marjorie realizes that, in working to improve her relationship with her mother, half the battle is being able to deal with her own anxieties, her own emotional processes built up over the years. Before we can fully make allowances for our mother's problems, we need to be able to see clearly which ones we are carrying into the relationship.

The difference our own state of emotional buoyancy makes to our relationship with our mother—which continues even after her death—can also be seen if that emotional state changes. Randall Laing's mother died some time ago; he was left with negative, even bitter, feelings about her. On the advice of a psychotherapist, he tried to overcome some of this emotional legacy by imagining that he was inviting his late parents back to his apartment and back into his life. "My shrink said, 'Why don't you invite them to your apartment?' I said, 'I don't think I want to do that,' and she said, 'They might be very impressed with it; they might think, "How wonderful for you."' So I actually pushed the elevator button, I said 'Hi,' and I showed them the apartment. We talked a little bit, and I took them through and showed them each room, and, as soon as I could, I got them out of the back door and never let them in again. I didn't want those people here."

At the time, the therapeutic experiment simply confirmed for him his negative feelings about his mother; but he now feels differently about her, mainly because he is happier in himself. "I sit in my wonderful apartment," he said, taking stock at his home in New York. "I have never been in demand so much as a writer, so I don't feel a failure. I'm older than I ever thought I would be, and my health—I'm not even knocking wood—is wonderful. So I don't really bitch about my mother now. She cannot control my happiness."

So we can see the effect on relationships when people

are feeling good about their lives: It becomes more possible to forgive, to look on the bright side, to let resentments drop away.

No matter how difficult we find our mother's behavior, it is important to remember that it is not her behavior per se that is causing us emotional distress: It is the way we feel about her behavior. It is more difficult to deal with your frustrations with her when you are not managing yourself very well. We need to feel emotionally secure to be able to overcome some of our frictions with our mother by seeing things from her perspective. To be able to successfully confront our mother about particular issues without alienating her or treating it like a sort of revenge, means feeling confident and calm. Only when you are able to feel reasonably at peace with yourself can you deal well with the dynamics of your relationship with your mother.

At the heart of managing your mother, then, is being able to accept yourself, with your own failings, for then you are more easily able to accept your mother, with all her flaws. And accepting your mother is a most important step toward achieving a better relationship with her.

> Above all, know yourself. Only when you feel at peace with yourself can you deal well with the dynamics of the relationship with your mother. If you can accept yourself with your flaws, you can accept her with her flaws.

The Ten Steps

Here are the ten steps once more:

1. Remember your mother's age.
2. Listen to your mother.
3. Remember that your mother has a past.
4. Ask your mother simply and directly how you can make her life better.
5. Ask your mother about your childhood history.
6. Get to know your mother's extended family.
7. Decide what personality trait you share with your mother.
8. If you find your mother difficult, confront the issues that divide you.
9. Keep a sense of humour about your mother.
10. Remember that managing your mother is really about managing yourself.

Your mother will always live inside you, whether she is causing a fuss or quietly helping your progress through life. One of my friends said this to me:

> We need someone to love,
> We need someone to hate,
> We need someone to survive,
> We need someone to blame.

Our mother can fit each of these needs. I hope that this book will help you to improve your relationship with your mother—and choose love.

Appendix

Questionnaire

Listed below are the questions we put to our interviewees about their relationship with their mother. You may wish to answer some of them for yourself. In our interviews, we were flexible in the order in which we put the questions, and we did not always ask every question. In responding to them yourself, it is important to remember that the questions are not a test; answer just those which seem to help you to articulate your memories and feelings.

How old are you and how old is your mother? or How old were you and how old was your mother when she died?

If she is still alive, how often do you see or talk to your mother?

What are your earliest and your fondest memories of your mother?

Is there any event that you feel marked a turning point in your relationship with your mother? Have there been different phases in your relationship, and what do you think caused them?

What is your area of greatest difficulty with your mother?

How would you describe your mother? How would she describe you?

What expectations does your mother have of you? And you of her?

What do you value most in your relationship with your mother?

If you could ask your mother any question and know she would answer truthfully, what would it be?

How much control do (or did) you think you have (had) in your relationship with your mother?

Would you change your mother, and if so, in what way? Would your mother (have) change(d) you, and in what way?

Do you love your mother? Does (did) she love you?

Has your mother influenced your choice of career?

Has she influenced your choice of relationships?

If you have brothers and/or sisters, how do their relationships with your mother compare with yours?

How would (did) you cope with your mother's death?

Do you share any personal characteristics with your mother?

Selected Bibliography

Amis, Kingsley. *The Folks That Live on the Hill*. London: Hutchinson, 1990.

Arcana, Judith. *Our Mothers' Daughters*. London: The Women's Press, 1981.

Bedell Smith, Sally. *Reflected Glory: The Life of Pamela Churchill Harriman*. New York: Simon & Schuster, 1996.

Bettelheim, Bruno. *The Uses of Enchantment: The Meaning and Importance of Fairy Tales*. New York: Vintage, 1989.

Borges, Jorge Luis. *Labyrinths: Selected Stories and Other Writings*. New York: W. W. Norton, 1966.

Bowlby, John. *Attachment and Loss*. Vol. 1, *Attachment*. London: Penguin Books, 1971.

———. *Attachment and Loss*. Vol. 3, *Sadness and Depression*. London: Penguin Books, 1981.

———. *Child Care and the Growth of Love*. London: Penguin Books, 1953.

Canfield, Jack, and Mark Victor Hansen. *Chicken Soup for the Soul*. Deerfield Beach, Fla.: Health Communications, 1993.

Canfield, Jack, Mark Victor Hansen, Jennifer Read Hawthorne, and Marci Shimoff. *Chicken Soup for the Woman's Soul*. Deerfield Beach, Fla: Health Communications, 1996.

Cardinal, Marie. *Words to Say It*. Cambridge, Mass.: Van Vactor & Goodheart, 1990.

Cloud, Henry, and John Townsend. *The Mom Factor*. Grand Rapids, Mich.: Zondervan Publishing House, 1998.

Coltart, Nina. *Slouching towards Bethlehem, and Further Psychoanalytic Explorations*. London: Other Press, 1998.

de Beauvoir, Simone. *Memoirs of a Dutiful Daughter*. Vol. 1, *Autobiography*. New York: Harper & Row, 1974.

Dryden, Windy, and Jack Gordon. *How to Cope with Difficult Parents*. London: Sheldon, 1995.

Edelman, Hope. *Letters from Motherless Daughters*. New York: Delta, 1995.

Erikson, Erik H. *Identity: Youth and Crisis*. New York: W. W. Norton, 1994.

Eyre, Richard. *Utopia and Other Places*. London: Bloomsbury Publishing Ltd, 1953.

Farrow, Mia. *What Falls Away: A Memoir*. New York: Doubleday, 1997.

Forna, Aminatta. *Mother of All Myths*. London: HarperCollins, 1998.

Forward, Susan. *Toxic Parents*. New York: Bantam, 1990.

Freud, Sigmund, and Joseph Breuer. *Studies on Hysteria*. London: The Hogarth Press, 1978.

Friday, Nancy. *My Mother, My Self*. New York: Delta, 1997.

———. *Women on Top*. New York: Pocket Books, 1993.

Gabbard, Krin, and Glen O. Gabbard, *Psychiatry and the Cinema*. Chicago: The University of Chicago Press, 1987.

Golden, Arthur. *Memoirs of a Geisha*. New York: Knopf, 1997.

Goleman, Daniel. *Emotional Intelligence*. New York: Bantam, 1997.

Golomb, Elan. *Trapped in the Mirror: Adult Children of Narcissists in Their Struggle for Self*. New York: Quill, 1995.

Grey Sexton, Linda. *Searching for Mercy Street: My Journey Back to My Mother*. Boston: Little, Brown & Co., 1994.

Harrison, Michael, and Christopher Stuart Clark, eds. *The New Dragon Book of Verse*. Oxford: Oxford University Press, 1977.

Hollway, Wendy, and Brid Featherstone. *Mothering and Ambivalence*. London: Routledge, 1997.

Horney, Karen. *Feminine Psychology*. New York: Norton, 1973.

Huffington, Arianna. *The Fourth Instinct: The Call of the Soul*. New York: Simon & Schuster, 1994.

Imber-Black, Evan. *The Secret Life of Families*. New York: Bantam, 1998.

Irving, John. *A Prayer for Owen Meany.* New York: Ballantine, 1990.

Jeffers, Susan. *Feel the Fear and Do It Anyway.* New York: Fawcett, 1992.

Jonas, Susan, and Marilyn Nissenson. *Friends for Life: Enriching the Bond Between Mothers and their Adult Daughters.* New York: Harcourt Brace, 1998.

Jung, C. G. *Memories, Dreams, Reflections.* New York: Vintage, 1989.

Kast, Verena. *Father/Daughter, Mother/Son.* Dorset: Element, 1997.

Keillor, Garrison. *Leaving Home.* New York: Penguin Books, 1988.

Kemp, Peter, ed. *The Oxford Dictionary of Literary Quotations.* New York: Oxford University Press, 1998.

Kiley, Dan. *The Peter Pan Syndrome: Men Who Have Never Grown Up.* New York: William Morrow, 1983.

Klein, Melanie. *Narrative of a Child Analysis: Envy and Gratitude and Other Works 1946–1963.* New York: Free Press, 1984.

——. *Love, Guilt and Reparation and Other Works 1921–1945.* New York: Free Press, 1984.

——. *The Psycho Analysis of Children.* New York: Free Press, 1984.

——. *Melanie Klein Today,* vol. 1. London: Routledge, 1988.

——. *Mainly Theory,* vol. 2. London: Routledge, 1988.

——. *Mainly Practice.* London: Routledge, 1988.

Kübler-Ross, Elisabeth. *On Death and Dying.* New York: Collier, 1997.

Lamott, Anne. *Bird by Bird.* New York: Anchor Books, 1995.

Larkin, Philip. *Collected Poems.* New York: Noonday Press, 1983.

Mah, Adeline Yen. *Falling Leaves.* New York: Broadway Books, 1997.

Mamet, David. *The Cabin.* New York: Vintage, 1993.

——. *Passover.* New York: St. Martin's, 1995.

Martin, Steve. *Wasp.* Los Angeles: Victoria Dailey Publisher, 1996.

McDougall, Joyce. *Theatres of the Mind: Illusion and Truth on the Psychoanalytic Stage.* London: Free Association Books, 1982.

McGoldrick, Monica, Carole M. Anderson, and Froma Walsh. *Women in Families: A Framework for Family Therapy.* New York: W. W. Norton, 1991.

Meltzer, Donald, M.D. *The Psycho-Analytical Process*. Strath Tay, Perthshire, Scotland: Clunie Press, 1979.

———. *Dream-Life, a Re-examination of Psycho-analytical Theory and Technique*. Edinburgh, Scotland: Clunie Press, 1984.

Miller, Lisa, Margaret Rustin, Michael Rustin, and Judy Shuttleworth. *Closely Observed Infants*. London: Gerald Duckworth, 1989.

Mitchell, Juliet, and Ann Oakley. *What Is Feminism?* Oxford: Basil Backwell, 1986.

Montagu, Ashley. *Growing Young*. Westport, Conn.: Bergin and Garvey, 1989.

Morrison, Mary C. *Let Evening Come: Reflections on Aging*. New York: Doubleday, 1998.

Munro, Alice. *Open Secrets*. New York: Vintage Books, 1994.

Nuland, Sherwin B. *How We Die: Reflections on Life's Final Chapter*. New York: Vintage, 1995.

Park, James. *Sons, Mothers and Other Lovers*. London: Little, Brown, 1995.

Parker, Rozsika. *Torn in Two: The Experience of Maternal Ambivalence*. London: Virago Press, 1995.

Peck, M. Scott. *The Road Less Traveled*. New York: Simon & Schuster, 1998.

Persaud, Raj. *Staying Sane: How to Make Your Mind Work for You*. London: Metro Books, 1998.

Pines, Dinora. *A Woman's Unconscious Use of Her Body*. New Haven: Yale University Press, 1994.

Pirandello, Luigi. *Naked*. London: Nick Hern Books, 1998.

Powell, Colin, with Joseph E. Persico. *My American Journey*. New York: Random House, 1995.

Quindlen, Anna. *One True Thing*. New York: Dell, 1998.

Racker, Heinrich. *Transference and Countertransference*. London: Maresfield, 1985.

Reinhold, Margret. *How to Survive in Spite of Your Parents: Coping with Hurtful Childhood Legacies*. London: Mandarin Paperbacks, 1991.

Rustin, Margaret, Maria Rhode, Alex Dubinsky, and Helene Dubinsky. *Tavistock Clinic Series*. London: Gerald Duckworth, 1997.

Rycroft, Charles. *A Critical Dictionary of Psychoanalysis*. New York: Penguin, 1995.

Sayers, Janet. *Mothers of Psychoanalysis*. New York: W. W. Norton, 1993.

———. *Boy Crazy*. London: Routledge, 1998.

Schectman, Jacqueline. *The Stepmother in Fairytales*. Boston: Sigo Press, 1993.

Sereny, Gitta. *Cries Unheard: The Story of Mary Bell*. New York: Owl, 2000.

Sheehy, Gail. *New Passages: Mapping Your Life Across Time*. New York: Ballantine, 1996.

Skynner, Robin, and John Cleese. *Life and How to Survive It*. New York: W. W. Norton, 1996.

St. James, Elaine. *Simplify Your Life*. New York: Hyperion, 1994.

Waddell, Margot. *Inside Lives: Psychoanalysis and the Growth of the Personality*. London: Gerald Duckworth, 1998.

Walker, Moira. *Women in Therapy and Counseling*. Milton Keynes, England: Open University Press, 1990.

Whitfield, Charles L., M.D. *Healing the Child Within*. Pompano Beach, Fla.: Health Communications, 1989.

Winterson, Jeanette. *Oranges Are Not the Only Fruit*. New York: Grove Press, 1997.

Wood Middlebrook, Diane. *Anne Sexton: A Biography*. New York: Random House, 1992.

Index